1995

MODERN
NATIONS
—OF THE—
WORLD

CANADA

MODERN
NATIONS
—OF THE—
WORLD

CANADA

BY JOHN F. GRABOWSKI

LUCENT BOOKS
P.O. BOX 289011
SAN DIEGO, CA 92198-9011

Library of Congress Cataloging-in-Publication Data

Grabowski, John F.
    Canada / by John Grabowski.
       p.   cm. — (Modern nations of the world)
    Includes bibliographical references (p.) and index.
    Summary: Examines the land, people, and history of Canada and
discusses its state of affairs and place in the world today.
    ISBN 1-56006-520-6 (alk. paper)
    1. Canada—Juvenile literature. [1. Canada.] I. Title.   II. Series.
F1008.2.G72 1998
971—dc21   97-40226
                                                                 CIP
                                                                  AC

CONTENTS

INTRODUCTION   6
   The Search for an Identity

CHAPTER ONE   9
   Taming the Land

CHAPTER TWO   27
   Toward a Modern Nation

CHAPTER THREE   43
   A Nation of Diversity

CHAPTER FOUR   64
   The Culture of Canada

CHAPTER FIVE   81
   Contemporary Canada

   Facts About Canada   93
   Chronology   96
   Suggestions for Further Reading   104
   Works Consulted   106
   Index   107
   Picture Credits   112
   About the Author   112

INTRODUCTION

THE SEARCH FOR AN IDENTITY

Rather than being a blend or "melting pot," the cultural composition of Canada is often compared to a mosaic, with the various pieces fitted together but still retaining their individual identities. The French and British, for example—the two largest groups—remain, arguably, as antagonistic to one another as their ancestors of two hundred years ago. A large segment of the French populace of Quebec still clamors for independence from Canada and for status as a separate nation. Communities of North American Indian tribes scattered throughout the nation are reluctant to live on government reserves, where they are expected to be thankful for handouts that those in power feel improve their previous "primitive" lifestyles. Many Inuit, who live on the tundra of the northern expanses, have resisted government attempts to force them to give up their nomadic existence and relocate in the "white man's" world. With these disparate ethnic affiliations fighting to hold on to their heritages, a Canadian identity has yet to emerge more than a century and a quarter after the country's Confederation. Yet Canada is a nation, though a nation held together by an unusual unity. As economist Kenneth Boulding once explained, "Canada has no cultural unity, no linguistic unity, no religious unity, no geographic unity. All it has is unity."

CANADA AND THE UNITED STATES

Being close neighbors with the United States has also hindered the development of a definitive Canadian identity. The majority of Canada's population lives within two hundred miles of the U.S. border. The United States is Canada's most important trading partner, and many Canadians feel dominated by American culture and economy. Sharing a border with the United States, remarked former prime minister Pierre Elliott Trudeau, is like "sleeping with an elephant. No

matter how friendly or even-tempered is the beast . . . one is affected by every twitch and grunt!"

REGIONAL IDENTITIES

The story of Canada is the story of how two historically opposed cultural groups, along with various native peoples, have come together to form a single contemporary entity, despite being spread out on a land of almost unimaginable size and geographic diversity. Without any single unifying cause to bring its peoples together—such as a struggle for freedom from an oppressive "motherland"—regional, rather than national, identities remain the norm. Canadians are likely to identify themselves as Ontarians or Quebecers rather than as Canadians. "There is Ontario patriotism, Quebec patriotism or western patriotism," said journalist and politician Henri Bourassa, "but there is no Canadian patriotism."

Despite perhaps overwhelming odds, Canadians have shaped for themselves a country that is respected and envied

Château Frontenac is a popular tourist site in Quebec City, where French and Canadian cultures coincide.

throughout the world. The United Nations Human Development Index has ranked Canada as the best place in the world to live on four separate occasions—1992, 1994, 1995, and 1996. The index is based on factors such as life expectancy, education, and health conditions. Canada's reputation for compassion and innovation is recognized internationally, as is its importance as a peaceful democratic nation. U.S. president Ronald Reagan acknowledged as much in 1985 when he said, "No other country in the world is more important to the United States than Canada, and we are blessed to have such a nation on our northern border."

The spirit, resolve, and tolerance exhibited by Canadians is responsible for the country's existence. It also ensures its survival in the future.

TAMING THE LAND

1

The first people to inhabit the wide-ranging expanse of land known today as Canada were prehistoric wanderers who migrated to the area approximately thirty thousand years ago. They came from eastern Asia at a time when the continent was connected to North America by the Bering land bridge. This strip of land, which joined modern-day Siberia and Alaska, was later submerged when melting ice raised the level of the oceans.

The descendants of these nomads spread eastward and southward across the vast continent, settling in different regions. Those who remained in the arctic north were the ancestors of the Inuit, or Eskimos, who live there today. The others, who ranged far and wide over the prairies of central Canada, were the forefathers of various tribes of Indians. Their societies were shaped in large part by the region of the continent in which they settled.

NATIVE CANADIANS

The Inuit are believed to have migrated across the mainland, north of the tree line, and settled in the area of Canada known today as the Yukon and Northwest Territories. This barren, isolated region consists of partly frozen land called tundra. Trees do not grow there, but assorted mosses, lichens, and shrubs may make an appearance during the brief summer growing season.

As with other prehistoric societies, the Inuit lifestyle was built around the search for food. They fished and caught seals along the coastlines, and hunted caribou and other game farther inland. The animals provided more than just food, however. Virtually every part of a carcass was utilized in some way, with the fur and skin being used for protection against the bitter cold and the bones and tendons for needles and thread.

Moving south, Canada's eastern forest area includes the Maritime Provinces of New Brunswick, Nova Scotia, Prince

Edward Island, and Newfoundland, as well as portions of southern Quebec. Woodland tribes, such as the Micmac, Beothuk, Cree, and Ojibwa, relied heavily on trees, constructing canoes that carried them through the lakes and rivers of the region. Hunting and fishing were necessary skills among these Algonquian-language tribes.

The southern Ontario vicinity, which includes the Saint Lawrence River valley, was home to the more sedentary tribes of the Iroquois alliance, such as the Mohawk, Oneida, Cayuga, and Seneca. The rich, fertile tract of land was perfect for farming, and crops replaced animals as the major portion of the native diet. The relative stability of this lifestyle saw nomadic practices give way to semipermanent settlements. Freed from the need to hunt and trap animals, these tribes had more time for other activities. Unfortunately, this included making war on neighboring settlements.

The most prominent feature of the Canadian terrain is the thousand-mile-wide swath of land surrounding Hudson Bay to the north of Ontario. Formed thousands of years ago by retreating glaciers, the landscape consists of thousands of

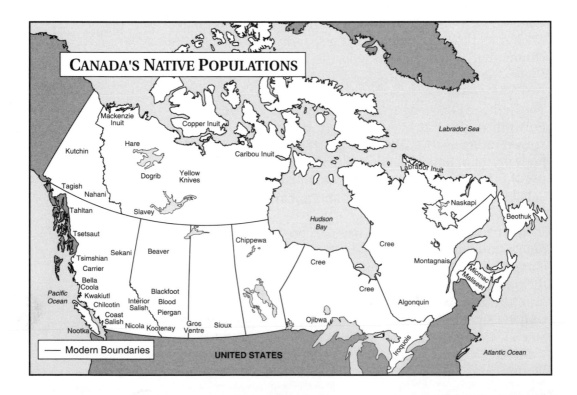

CANADA'S NATIVE POPULATIONS

lakes dotting the generally inhospitable terrain, which is rich in mineral wealth. Stretching west, the shield turns into the prairies of northern Manitoba, Saskatchewan, and Alberta. To the Plains Indians, like the Blackfoot, Blood, Piergan, Cree, and Sioux, horses were valuable assets on these open expanses. Through cooperative efforts, herds of roaming buffalo could be captured by native riders. When these slain beasts were brought back to the natives' teepee villages, virtually every part of their bodies was used in some manner, be it for food, clothing, tools, or fuel.

The area to the west of the central plains, consisting of present-day British Columbia, is known as the Western Cordillera (Spanish for "mountain range"). Tribes native to the region included the Kootenay, Lillooet, and Shushwap. These tribes scoured the woodlands, hunting deer and goats and collecting berries. Products made from trees were used extensively, and wooden structures often replaced the animal-skin teepees that were prevalent on the plains.

Closer to the western coastline, tribes such as the Haida, Bella Coola, Nootka, and coast Salish relied on the sea for their food. Sea otters, sea lions, and whales played important roles in the lives of the natives. Most important, however, was the salmon. Some of the Pacific tribes even thought salmon were supernatural creatures who changed into fish to offer themselves as sustenance for human beings.

THE FIRST EUROPEANS:
THE ARRIVAL OF THE VIKINGS

It was not until about A.D. 1000 that Europeans touched down on the shores of North America. Norse sagas relate the tale of Eric Thorvaldson, better known as Eric the Red, who sailed from Iceland and found Greenland. From there, his son, Leif Ericson, sailed west to the shores of Newfoundland. Most historians believe this to be the first landing made by Europeans on the continent. In the 1960s a small Viking settlement was unearthed at L'Anse-aux-Meadows on the island of Newfoundland. The archaeological discovery of this Norse site appears to substantiate this theory.

Due to the small number of settlers and the lack of means for suppressing the natives, the Vikings abandoned their community after a few years. It would be four hundred more years before European explorers again touched down in Canada.

Christopher Columbus set foot in the New World in 1492 and inspired other explorers to follow.

It was Christopher Columbus's voyage to the "New World" in 1492 that spurred interest among other explorers to sail the Atlantic. One of those men, Italian navigator John Cabot (born Giovanni Caboto), was commissioned by King Henry VII of England to search for a northern route to the Far East, in a quest for gold, jewels, and valuable spices. Setting out on May 2, 1497, he soon reached the eastern coast of Canada somewhere between Newfoundland and Nova Scotia and claimed the land for England. Although he did not return home with the hoped-for riches from the Orient, he reported sailing through waters thick with fish. This aroused interest in other countries, such as France and Portugal, which sent expeditions to partake of the sea's abundance.

In another effort to find a passage to the Far East, King Francis I of France sent Jacques Cartier on three voyages to the New World. On his first trip in 1534, he located the mouth of the Saint Lawrence River and landed on Gaspé Peninsula, at the site of present-day New Brunswick. He claimed the land for France and erected a thirty-foot cross there.

The next year, Cartier sailed up the river to the Iroquois village of Stadacona (the future site of Quebec City). At this point of his trip, he went ashore to speak with the natives. He asked them what the area was called. Thinking he meant the immediate village, they told him "kanata," which was the Iroquois word for "settlement," or "collection of houses." The French proceeded to use the name Canada to apply to the surrounding area and, later, to the entire country.

THE FRENCH FUR TRADE

In the ensuing years, the French continued to fish the plentiful waters along the eastern coast. In order to keep their fish from rotting on the return trip home, the crews dried their catches on racks set up on the shore. When neighboring tribes of Indians came by, the fishermen would trade manufactured goods, such as knives, tools, and kettles, for beaver

French explorer Jacques Cartier first had contact with Canada's Iroquois Indians in 1535.

Samuel de Champlain explored the Canadian wilderness, established the settlement of Quebec in 1608, and expanded the French fur trade.

pelts from the natives. The pelts were a prized commodity, and beaver-skin hats became all the rage in Europe during the sixteenth century.

King Henry IV of France made plans to establish a colony in the New World. New France would organize and stabilize the new fur trade, ensuring a steady source of income for the homeland. Henry's plans became a reality on July 3, 1608, when explorer Samuel de Champlain established the first successful permanent French settlement in Canada at the confluence of the Saint Lawrence and Saint Charles Rivers. Champlain named the settlement Quebec, which was apparently the Algonquian word for a sudden narrowing of the water, or strait, such as that near the settlement's location. Champlain's men befriended the Algonquian and Huron Indians of the region, trading for furs and other supplies. They allied themselves with these Indians in their battles with nearby Mohawk and Iroquois tribes.

Champlain continued his explorations, pushing farther into the heart of the continent. He discovered the great lake that today bears his name and expanded the French fur-trade network. Through his efforts, Jesuit missionaries were brought over to introduce Christianity to the natives in 1625. Unfortunately, despite his efforts, the colony had difficulty attracting settlers, in large part due to the harsh winter climate. The small population made the colony vulnerable to attacks by Iroquois and to the intrusion of British settlers.

ENGLISH CLAIMS

English explorers like Martin Frobisher and Henry Hudson had continued the search for a northern passage to the Far East. Frobisher explored the area around Baffin Bay on three voyages in the 1570s. In 1610 Hudson pushed west of the bay through the northern ice fields until he came upon an enormous body of water. Fearing that Hudson desired to

go farther into the harsh and dangerous territory, with its
freezing temperatures and huge masses of floating ice, his
crew mutinied and cast him adrift to die in the bay that now
bears his name.

England had long been interested in the Saint Lawrence
region, primarily because of the fishing industry. By 1625 the
English had landed in what is now the United States and
were establishing colonies to the south and east in New England, New York, Pennsylvania, New Jersey, Delaware, Mary-
land, and Virginia. With the boundaries between the French
and British claims never fully defined, the English were gradually able to advance into French territory, increasing tensions between the two groups.

In 1627 the French government passed control of New
France to the Company of New France, commonly referred
to as the Company of the Hundred Associates because of the
number of its shareholders. The company was formed for the
purpose of carrying on trade in the New World and increasing New France's population by four hundred settlers a year.

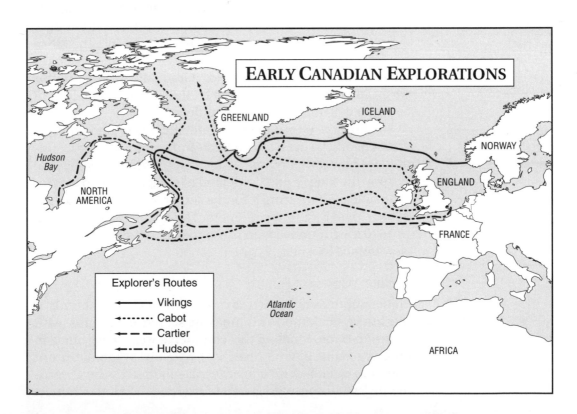

Within a year, however, war broke out in Europe between France and England. British forces in the New World attacked French settlements in Canada, and Quebec City was captured in 1629. Champlain was taken prisoner and sent to England.

The settlement was returned to the French in 1632 under the terms of the Treaty of Saint-Germain-en-Laye, and the Hundred Associates retook possession the following year. Champlain returned to New France as governor in 1633, and fur trading soon resumed.

A WARD OF THE CROWN

Things did not go smoothly for the company, however. In 1647 a new governing council was established by order of the king of France. The council allowed the citizens of New France a limited amount of representation in their government. This assembly was not particularly competent, however, and in 1663 King Louis XIV made New France a crown colony. With France once again making all the decisions, the brief experiment of partial self-autonomy came to an end.

Troops were sent to the royal province to defend the settlers against both the Iroquois—who had inflicted a series of defeats on the Huron and now controlled the Indian side of the fur trade—and the English, who had continued to make inroads into the New World. Gradually, the superior weaponry of the troops convinced the Indians of the folly of continued hostilities with the settlers.

Through the efforts of Jean Talon, the first intendant (government official in charge of trade and administration), hundreds of new settlers came to the region. Under a seigneurial system, the king would grant land to a seigneur, who was responsible for preparing it for the settlers to use. The settlers, in turn, paid rent to the seigneur. The system was a success; by 1676 the fur trade again prospered, and the population of New France had nearly tripled.

COMPETITION FOR FURS

French fur traders, known as *coureurs de bois* ("vagabonds of the forest"), roamed the areas in search of Indians with whom to trade. Much of this commerce was illegal, since in order to avoid paying taxes, many of the traders did not bother to obtain trading licenses, as required by the government. Two of these disgruntled traders—Médard Chouart

des Groseilliers and Pierre Esprit Radisson—transferred their
loyalties to England.

In 1670 Groseilliers led a small party of traders into the region around Hudson Bay and then returned to England with
a shipment of pelts. King Charles II granted a charter to the
party to form the Hudson's Bay Company. The charter established the company as a British outpost in the valuable wa-
tershed area by granting it a trade monopoly and the right to
rule all the land draining into the huge bay. The region became known as Rupert's Land in honor of King Charles's
nephew, Prince Rupert, who was a member of the party.

Conflicts between the French and English in Europe had
been going on for many years. With the Hudson's Bay Colony
to the north and the thirteen American colonies to the south,
New France was being hemmed in by its enemies. The
French were forced to push farther west into the interior in
pursuit of the valued pelts.

Explorers like Robert Cavelier, Sieur de La Salle, and missionaries like Jacques Marquette roamed far inland in an

*In a dining hall at Port
Royal, French colonists
feast and mingle with
native Indians.*

In this print entitled "Revels of the Indians at a French Fort," French settlers and Pontiac Indians dance together as wary English intruders (pictured right) look on. While the French learned to live as neighbors with the natives, tensions between France and England kept the European settlers at odds.

effort to expand the colony's borders and spread Christianity. Settlers left Quebec and moved through the Great Lakes region and into the Ohio and Mississippi River valleys. All areas they visited were claimed in the name of France. By the late part of the seventeenth century, the French network of trading posts extended as far north as Hudson Bay and as far west as the central plains of present-day Canada.

CLASH OF EMPIRES

In 1689 King William III of England entered the War of the Grand Alliance—the first of a new series of conflicts with France in Europe. These wars were mirrored in North America by four battles between the English and French. In the first, the French, joined by their Indian allies, attacked the British outposts near Hudson Bay, in New England, and in New York. The British responded with attacks on French settlements. In 1697 the Treaty of Ryswick ended hostilities in Europe, and both sides returned to their original holdings in the New World. Tensions between the two, however, remained high, and attacks continued on each other's settlements.

From 1702 to 1713, the War of the Spanish Succession saw England oppose Spain and France. Queen Anne's War was its North American counterpart. Suffering defeat in Europe, France signed the Treaty of Utrecht, which required that France surrender its claims to Newfoundland, the Hudson Bay area, and all of Acadia (renamed Nova Scotia), except for Isle Royale (now known as Cape Breton Island). The period following the war was one of relative peace and stability. Determined to prevent any further losses to the British, the governors of New France built a series of fortified posts, including an imposing stronghold at Louisbourg

LOUIS DE BUADE, COMTE DE FRONTENAC

In 1689, as the War of the Grand Alliance raged in Europe, the colony of New France was being menaced by British military garrisons. Taking the offensive, the governor-general of the colony, Louis de Buade, Comte de Frontenac, mounted a series of attacks that spread fear throughout the British forces. The British responded by sending a fleet of warships to capture New France. Frontenac gathered French troops at Quebec to meet the incoming ships under the command of Admiral William Phips.

On October 16, 1690, Phips sent Major Savage as his emissary, ordering Frontenac to surrender the town in order to avoid a bloody onslaught. Frontenac had Savage blindfolded upon landing and proceeded to bring him to his headquarters. By creating a great commotion, French citizens and soldiers in the streets gave Major Savage the impression that the townspeople were ready and able to defend the city. Responding to the British orders, Frontenac told Savage, "My only reply to your general will be from the mouth of my cannons!" He had convinced the British messenger that the French troops were greater in size, stronger, and better prepared than they actually were.

The emissary was returned to his ship and relayed the message to Admiral Phips. When the fourteen thousand British troops landed on the opposite shore the next day, they were rebuffed by fewer than five hundred Canadian soldiers. After three days of confrontation, the British retreated, leaving behind five of their six artillery pieces. Frontenac's grand deception was a success.

on Cape Breton Island. Regardless, British traders and settlers moved into French territory, and tensions once more were heightened.

The onset of the War of the Austrian Succession in Europe (1740) was reflected in the confrontation known as King George's War (1744–1748) in the Americas. The most meaningful action of the war was the capture of Louisbourg by the British in 1745. Louisbourg guarded the mouth of the Saint Lawrence River, the major waterway into the Canadian interior. The French received the fortress back as part of the Treaty of Aix-la-Chapelle, which ended the war in 1748. The British, however, were now determined to expel their enemy from the continent.

It did not take long for the two adversaries to begin preparing for a final round of hostilities. Both sides advanced

THE EVACUATION OF THE ACADIANS

For many years, the British challenged the claims of the French to the area known as Acadia. As one of the terms of the Treaty of Utrecht, which ended the War of the Spanish Succession, the French surrendered most of their stake in the region to the British, who referred to it as Nova Scotia.

Some ten thousand French who lived in Acadia, however, refused to take the oath of allegiance to the British Crown, claiming neutrality. These peaceful people did not resist the British but only wished to preserve their pastoral existence.

Fearing possible problems in the future, Charles Lawrence, the governor of Nova Scotia, ordered those Acadians who refused to swear loyalty transported to the English-speaking colonies in the American South. Numerous harmless peasant families were broken up, as eight thousand Acadians were shipped out by boat in 1755. The man in charge of the operation, Colonel John Winslow, described the poignant evacuation in the October 8, 1755, entry to his journal (as quoted in *The Canadians,* by George Woodcock):

October 8th. Began to Embarke the Inhabitants who [departed] unwillingly, the women in Great Distress Carrying off their children in their arms. Others carrying their Decript [decrepit] Parents in their Carts and all their Goods Moving in great Confusion & appeard a Scene of Woe & Diestress.

Although a few would later return to their homeland, the majority of the Acadians settled in current-day Louisiana. The descendants of the exiles are the people known today as Cajuns. Henry Wadsworth Longfellow's celebrated poem "Evangeline" was inspired by this mass exodus.

farther into the Ohio Valley toward the strategic location known as the Forks.

THE FRENCH AND INDIAN WAR

When the Seven Years' War between France and England exploded in Europe, it was paralleled by the French and Indian War in North America. The British, with the aid of their Iroquois allies, attacked and captured one fortress after another, including Louisbourg, which gave them control of the entrance to the Saint Lawrence River. Quebec and the other French inland settlements could no longer depend on receiving supplies from France.

The British realized that the capture of Quebec was critical to the defeat of the French. The pivotal battle on the Plains of Abraham saw the British troops of General James Wolfe attack the French forces of General Louis Joseph de Montcalm on the morning of September 13, 1759. When the smoke had cleared, the French army had fled in retreat. The city of Quebec surrendered on September 18.

The war dragged on awhile longer, however, and it was not until Montreal fell the following year that the conquest—*La Conquête* to the French—was complete. The memory of this defeat fires up French Canadian nationalism even to the present day.

The capture of the French settlement of Quebec on September 13, 1759, was a victory for the English forces during the French and Indian War.

After Quebec (pictured) fell under British rule, the Crown issued the Quebec Act of 1774 to calm the fears of the French citizens. The act expanded Quebec's borders and guaranteed religious freedom to the populace.

In 1763 the French signed the Treaty of Paris, surrendering most of their claims in the New World to England. Under the provisions of the pact, Britain also received Florida from Spain, while Spain was given New Orleans and much of France's claim to land west of the Mississippi River. The only territory France was allowed to keep were the islands of Saint Pierre and Miquelon in the Gulf of St. Lawrence, which they maintain to the present day. For all intents and purposes, French rule in the New World was at an end.

UNDER ENGLISH RULE

Upon taking possession of France's colonies in the New World, the British renamed New France the colony of Quebec. The English were faced with the immediate problem of how to govern their new citizens. An attempt was made to Anglicize the populace, but the French viewed this as a threat to their identity and culture. This fear of assimilation can still be sensed in Quebec today.

Realizing the necessity of maintaining good relations with the French Canadians, England passed the Quebec Act of 1774. Among other things, it guaranteed the French religious freedom and extended Quebec's borders into the fertile Ohio Valley. The English system of criminal law was adopted, but French civil law was retained.

This act aroused anger and resentment in the American colonies, where it was viewed as a British attempt to limit westward expansion. With animosity toward the British at its height, the American Revolution followed in short order.

Not all Americans sided with the Revolutionaries, however. Thousands of English Loyalists moved north into Nova Scotia. The creation of the colony of New Brunswick in 1784 is one of the results of this immigration.

Other Loyalists fled to Quebec, where antagonism grew between the newly arrived British Protestants and the French Catholics. This eventually led to the division of Quebec into Upper Canada (present-day Ontario) and Lower Canada (present-day Quebec) in 1791. Both were ruled by lieutenant governors and legislative assemblies appointed by Britain. French customs and institutions, however, prevailed in Lower Canada.

WESTWARD EXPANSION

During this period of transformation, fur trading continued to be an important facet of Canadian life. The Montreal-based North West Company emerged as a challenger to the

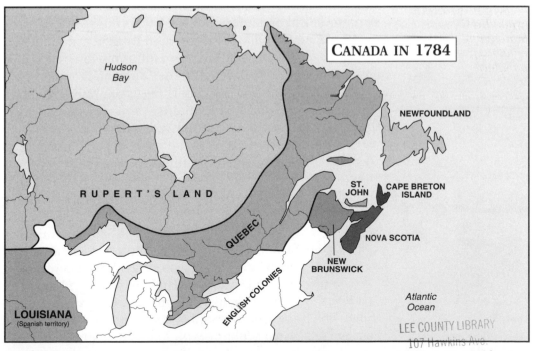

mighty Hudson's Bay Company in 1784. The competition between the two led to new explorations to the west and north of the Great Lakes region. Alexander Mackenzie, one of the partners in the North West Company, became obsessed with the idea of finding a waterway to the Pacific Ocean. In 1789 he traveled the river that now bears his name and eventually reached the Arctic Ocean. Four years later he reached the Pacific on another one of his forays, making him the first European to travel the breadth of Canada. The early 1800s saw adventurers like Simon Fraser and David Thompson follow in his footsteps, and settlements in the western region slowly began to develop.

The British-American rivalry in the fur trade was one of the main issues that led to the War of 1812, together with British interference with American shipping lanes. The Americans, expecting to find supporters above the border, invaded Canada but were turned back by the British and their Indian allies.

The war eventually ended in a stalemate, with neither side forced to make concessions. The boundary between British North America and the United States east of the Mississippi was confirmed, however, and this induced a feeling of separateness between the countries. The development of a sense of nationalism and unity could be felt among the Canadians. A definite, albeit weak, Canadian patriotism began to emerge.

During the period following the war, Britain tried to strengthen its Canadian colonies by encouraging and assisting immigration. Approximately eight hundred thousand people came over between the years 1815 and 1850, with most settling in the relatively uncleared tracts of present-day Ontario.

TWO NATIONS IN A SINGLE STATE

As the population increased, so, too, did dissatisfaction with the political institutions. Canadians began to clamor for increased participation in the colony's affairs, claiming the British Crown exerted too much influence. In Lower Canada, an unsuccessful revolt was led by Louis Joseph Papineau in 1837. The next year William Lyon Mackenzie did likewise in

Looking for a waterway to the Pacific, Alexander Mackenzie was the first European explorer to travel the breadth of Canada.

Upper Canada. Although both rebellions were put down, nineteen-year-old Queen Victoria sent John Lambton, the first earl of Durham, to further investigate the grievances of the rebels. In his famous report of 1839, Durham recommended uniting Upper and Lower Canada and establishing the concept of "responsible government." Under this system, the government leader must be held accountable to an elected legislative assembly. Durham made note of the chasm that separated the English and the French: "I have found two nations warring within the bosom of a single state; I found a struggle, not of principles, but of races."

Two years later his recommendations were acted upon. Through the Act of Union, the provinces of Upper and Lower Canada were united as the Province of Canada under a single legislature, with each region having equal representation. The colony would govern itself in local matters, but the British Crown would continue to rule over all other affairs.

The new government was not a rousing success. No single party could attract enough backing from both French- and English-speaking voters to gain a majority in the legislature. With frequent changes of leadership, the province's economic and social development was significantly impeded.

A reciprocal trade agreement in 1854 led to closer relations with the United States, as did the development of the railroad system. The Grand Trunk Railway, linking Montreal and Toronto, brought the provinces closer together and helped to encourage the development of cities, changes that would forever transform Canadian society.

CONFEDERATION

The outbreak of the American Civil War in 1861, however, heightened tensions in Canada. Because England backed the South during the war, Canadians feared that U.S. government troops might attempt to seize British colonies north of the border. Canadians recognized the need for a government that could provide a strong defense. In addition, it should be one that would press for the development of the railroad system and encourage the development of the western region. All signs pointed toward a desire for Canadian unity.

An important step toward this union of the Canadian colonies, called Confederation, was taken in 1864 when John A. Macdonald, George Brown, and George Étienne Cartier—

LAURA SECORD, THE CANADIAN PAUL REVERE

Following the onset of the War of 1812, opposing forces struggled to gain control of the waterways in the Great Lakes region. One of the British subjects living in the area was Laura Ingersoll Secord, a thirty-seven-year-old Loyalist from Massachusetts whose family had immigrated to Canada when she was just a child. Although born in the United States, she was fiercely loyal to the British Crown. Laura was the wife of James Secord, a Queenston settler who had been wounded six months earlier at the Battle of Queenston Heights.

On the evening of June 21, 1813, American soldiers forced their way into the Secord home and demanded food. As the evening progressed, the young woman overheard a Colonel Boerstter speak of making "a surprise move against FitzGibbon at Beaver Dams." Dressed as a milkmaid, she bravely traipsed nineteen miles though American lines. She arrived at the British garrison just in time to warn Lieutenant James FitzGibbon of the planned American offensive at the Niagara frontier in Upper Canada.

Although it has been theorized that FitzGibbon had previously been alerted by his Indian spies and already knew of the plans, this does not in any way diminish Secord's heroic deed. Had she been caught, she would probably have been put to death. Her action secured a place for her in Canadian history as her country's Paul Revere.

leaders of the rival Conservative, Liberal, and Reformer Parties in the Province of Canada—formed a coalition. Representatives of the Maritime Provinces—New Brunswick, Nova Scotia, Prince Edward Island, and Newfoundland—were meeting in Charlottetown, Prince Edward Island, in a historic conference where the concept of Maritime unity was being discussed. Macdonald and Brown "crashed" the conference and persuaded the others to postpone their plans and consider the concept of Confederation.

Despite some setbacks, a delegation of Canadians arrived in London three years later to meet with British leaders. Together, they drew up the British North America Act, which would serve as Canada's constitution until 1982. On July 1, 1867, the provinces of Ontario, Quebec, Nova Scotia, and New Brunswick were united (Prince Edward Island and Newfoundland rejected union), and the Dominion of Canada became a reality.

Toward a
Modern Nation

2

The new Dominion of Canada was still a colony of England. It created a parliamentary system of government similar to the one that existed in Britain. An appointed Senate and an elected House of Commons were presided over by a British governor-general. The prime minister was the leader of the party with the most members in Parliament. With the Conservative Party in the majority, John A. Macdonald was appointed as the Dominion's first prime minister in 1867. He would remain in this position until his death in 1891, except for the five-year period from 1873 to 1878 when he lost to a Liberal candidate.

The Confederation Expands

One of Macdonald's goals was to expand Canada's western border. It was feared that the Americans to the south would move into the uncharted wilderness and attempt to claim the land.

Although the original Dominion consisted of just four provinces—Ontario (Canada West, or Upper Canada), Quebec (Canada East, or Lower Canada), Nova Scotia, and New Brunswick—the British North America Act of 1867 had provided for the future admission of other regions, including the land owned by the Hudson's Bay Company, known as Rupert's Land. But first, title to the land had to be obtained from the company. The purchase of this region—which included most of present-day Manitoba and parts of Saskatchewan, Alberta, and the Northwest Territories—was completed in 1869. The Canadian government paid the company the equivalent of $1.5 million for the region and renamed it the Northwest Territories.

The Métis Rebellions

Overlooked in the purchase of Rupert's Land were the rights of the Métis. The Métis were mostly descendants of French fur traders who had married native women and settled in the

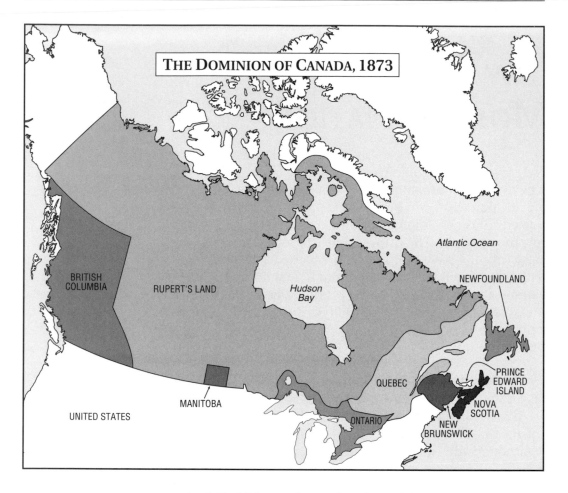

region's Red River colony. They feared that their lifestyle and land claims would be threatened by British Protestant settlers. When surveyors were sent in to map the area, the Métis, led by Louis Riel, prevented them from doing so. Riel became the leader of a provisional government set up at Fort Garry (present-day Winnipeg). Negotiations with the Canadian government resulted in the settlement being admitted into the Confederation in 1870 as the province of Manitoba.

That same year, however, Riel approved the execution of Thomas Scott, a Protestant who had plotted to assassinate him. Canadians in Scott's native Ontario were angered and called for Riel's capture, but French Canadians in Quebec sided with the Métis. Prime Minister Macdonald sent soldiers to arrest Riel, but the Métis leader fled across the border to Montana before he could be apprehended.

Despite having won a victory with the acceptance of Manitoba as a province, the Métis were still frustrated with the increased number of settlers moving into the area. Many sold their land and moved west toward the Saskatchewan River. Government surveyors followed, and in 1885 Riel was again called upon to help them retain their rights to the land. This time Riel was captured and tried for Scott's execution of fifteen years before. He was found guilty and hanged, incurring the wrath of Quebecers and increasing the tensions between the French and British Canadians.

THE CANADIAN PACIFIC RAILWAY

On the western coast, placer gold deposits (fragments or flakes found mixed with loose sand or gravel, rather than in veins) had been discovered along the Fraser River in 1858. Prospectors flocked to the area, many from California, and two colonies were established—Vancouver Island and British Columbia. As gold activity in the region waned, the two colonies united to become one. It was this colony of British Columbia that Macdonald hoped to persuade to join the Confederation. To do so, he promised British Columbians that a railway would be constructed to connect the colony

Métis traders (pictured here circa 1872) feared losing their land and lifestyle to the increasing waves of English settlers who moved westward through Canada.

with the east. The offer was accepted, and British Columbia became the sixth province in the Dominion in 1871. The colony of Prince Edward Island on the Atlantic coast joined two years later as the seventh province. The new country now stretched from the Atlantic Ocean to the Pacific.

Right from the start, construction of the promised railway ran into difficulties. Financial and management problems led to corruption charges against Macdonald's government. As a result, he resigned as prime minister in 1873. His successor, Alexander Mackenzie of the Liberal Party, fared no better. With completion of the project threatened, Macdonald was reelected in 1878. Physical obstacles—such as blasting through mountains and constructing bridges over rivers— were overcome, and the final spike was driven on November

THE ROYAL CANADIAN MOUNTED POLICE

With further western expansion a reality, it was only a matter of time until a police force became a necessity for the country. In 1873—six years after Confederation—the North-West Mounted Police was formed in response to requests from the Plains Indians. Whiskey traders in the area had been creating trouble among the tribes, and native leaders were seeking help to curb the lawlessness. When several native children and women were killed in a dispute between hunters and Assiniboin Indians in May of that year, the requests were finally acted upon.

On July 8, 1874, a contingent consisting of 275 officers and men, together with wagons, carts, cattle, horses, oxen, farm machinery, field guns, and mortars, began the famous March West from Fort Dufferin, Manitoba, to the foothills of the Rocky Mountains, where they established Fort Macleod. Committed to patrolling three hundred thousand square miles of wilderness, the red-jacketed "Mounties" earned the respect of both natives and settlers for their persistence, bravery, and strict but fair enforcement of the laws of the land.

In 1904, in recognition of its work, the word "Royal" was added to the force's name. Sixteen years later, the force absorbed the Dominion Police and was renamed the Royal Canadian Mounted Police. Today the RCMP numbers more than twenty thousand men and women. While it is Canada's federal police force, it also provides provincial policing for all the provinces, except Ontario and Quebec.

Canadian Mounties are still an active part of law enforcement in the country's hinterlands and even in its urban areas.

7, 1885, at Craigellachie, British Columbia. The eastern and western regions of the Dominion were linked at last.

WILFRID LAURIER

John Macdonald died in 1891, and by 1896 the Conservative Party had fallen from power. With the backing of a large majority in Quebec, Liberal Wilfrid Laurier became the first French Canadian to hold the office of prime minister. He shared Macdonald's views on settling the west and offered free farmland to European immigrants. Laurier's plan was a great success, and more than two million new settlers arrived by the early 1900s. With the completion of the transcontinental railroad, the prairies of the west were now more easily accessible, and farming became an attractive lifestyle. New strains of wheat better suited to Canada's climate were developed. Wheat became Canada's leading export crop in what is known as the Golden Age of Laurier.

John Macdonald served as the first prime minister of the Dominion of Canada. His political agenda included expanding Canada's western border and stimulating the nation's industry

The economy received another boost with the development of the mining industry in the Northwest Territories. Canada's vast mineral wealth had been hinted at when nickel was discovered near Sudbury, Ontario, in 1883. When gold was discovered in 1896 on Klondike Creek in the Yukon, thousands of prospectors poured into the region, many from the United States. The influx of adventurers and miners gave a needed assist to an economy that had been suffering through a depression since 1873.

Part of the reason for that depression had been the so-called National Policy of John Macdonald. In an effort to encourage Canadian business, Macdonald put a tariff on cheaper merchandise entering the country from the United States. Laurier wanted trade barriers dropped and a policy of reciprocity adopted. This meant there would be no tax on goods from either country that were sold in the other. Laurier eventually negotiated such a policy with the United States. However, when it was presented to the people, there was strong opposition to it from the segment of the population that resented American influence in Canadian affairs. This became one of the main issues leading to the defeat of the Conservative Party in the election of 1911. Laurier's term as prime minister, the longest continuous term in Canadian history, came to an end.

CANADA IN WORLD WAR I

In 1914, at the time of the outbreak of World War I in Europe, Canada was still a subject of the British Empire. As such, it entered the war against Germany on Britain's side. Thousands of Canadians volunteered for military service as the country pooled its resources for the war effort. Within months thirty-three thousand Canadian troops were on their way overseas, many never to return home. Canadian forces distinguished themselves at several battles, including those at Ypres, Belgium, and Vimy Ridge, France.

Unfortunately, the casualty count was high. Replacements were needed, but the number of volunteers had dropped sharply. Laurier's successor as prime minister, Conservative Robert Borden, proposed mandatory military conscription—a draft—to the electorate in the 1917 elections. Although English Canadians generally supported the proposal, French Canadians were vehemently opposed to it, as most did not feel the strong ties to the motherland that English Canadians did. Borden carried the election in every province except Quebec, as French Canadian resentment once again reared its head.

By the time the war was over, more than six hundred thousand Canadians had served, and nearly sixty thousand had lost their lives. Economically, Canada's position in the world community had been strengthened, as the demand for ships, shells, and other equipment gave the steel industry a tremendous boost. Borden, who had become more and more dissatisfied with Canada's status as a colony, demanded—and received—more of a voice in international affairs. When the war ended, Canada signed the Treaty of Versailles on its own behalf. It also obtained membership in the League of Nations, the new organization formed in 1920 to act as an international peacekeeping body.

CANADA BETWEEN WARS

The period immediately following World War I was a relatively prosperous time for most Canadians. Problems soon arose, however, on the labor front. With increased production as a result of the war effort, union membership surged. Afterward, as veterans began returning to the workforce, unemployment also climbed, as there simply were not enough jobs for everyone. Labor union leaders began lobbying for higher wages and collective bargaining, and a rift soon developed between management and workers. The unrest came to an ugly head with the Winnipeg General Strike of 1919.

What began on May 15 as a strike by workers in the building and metal trades soon escalated until the whole city of Winnipeg was brought to a standstill. In an unfortunate confrontation with the Royal Canadian Mounted Police, one person was killed and thirty injured. Leaders of the strike were arrested, convicted of sedition (conduct inciting rebellion against the authority of the state), and imprisoned. The strike finally ended on June 25, but the bitterness that had been created took years to mend.

 ## ROBERT HENDERSON AND THE KLONDIKE GOLD RUSH

Discovering gold and striking it rich had been the dream of Robert Henderson for many years. Raised in Nova Scotia, he searched for the precious metal in the hills of Colorado for several years before trekking north to the Alaska-Canada border. It was there, in the summer of 1896, that he came across several flakes of gold while panning in a small creek near the Yukon River. Henderson eventually unearthed $750 worth of nuggets from the creek that he christened Gold Bottom. The fortune he sought, however, was not to be his.

Returning to his camp one day, Henderson met up with George Washington Carmack and his two Indian companions—Skookum Jim and Tagish Charlie—who were hunting in the region. As was the code of honor among pioneers of the day, Henderson told Carmack about his strike. However, like many people of the time, Henderson felt Indians were inferior to whites. His disdain for the native pair was obvious, and the three hunters left, incensed at Henderson's behavior.

Several days later, while camping at nearby Rabbit Creek, one member of the trio found a gold nugget in the clear water. Euphoric, Carmack proceeded to file claims for the three in the town of Fortymile. He freely shared information about his strike, and the citizens of Fortymile rushed to stake claims and share in the great wealth.

Carmack, however, did not tell Henderson of his find, even though it was located less than a mile from Henderson's campsite. Although there is no way of knowing why he failed to do so, the generally accepted theory is that it was in reaction to Henderson's treatment of Carmack's two Indian companions.

Robert Henderson continued to pan for gold for the rest of his days. He died in 1933, his hopes for a major strike dying with him.

The economy continued to prosper in the early 1920s as William Lyon Mackenzie King and the Liberal Party came into power. King's objectives were simple: Keep Canada united, and help it become independent of Great Britain. Toward these ends, he clashed with the British Crown on several occasions. In 1926 King traveled to London to attend a conference with representatives from the other British dominions and from the British government. As a result of this meeting, the British Commonwealth of Nations was formed, with the dominions winning status as equal members. Together with Canada, several members of the Commonwealth finally won recognition as independent nations when the British Parliament enacted the Statute of Westminster on December 11, 1931.

Canadian soldiers train for trench warfare during World War I. As a nation still tied to the British Crown, Canada entered the war as England's ally, offering six hundred thousand troops to the cause.

Unfortunately, the Great Depression had hit the new nation with full force, bringing prosperity to a grinding halt. The New York Stock Market crash of October 1929 sent reverberations that were felt around the world, and particularly in Canada. Since the economies of the United States and other Canadian trading partners were collapsing, the market for Canadian natural resources and manufactured

A FAMOUS MASCOT

During World War I, Captain Harry Colebourn of the 34th Regiment of Cavalry was on his way to England to join the 2nd Canadian Infantry Brigade. While crossing Canada, his train made a stop at White River, Ontario. It was there that Colebourn made the acquaintance of a hunter who had killed a female bear and was in possession of the bear's cub. Colebourn bought the cub and named it Winnie, after his hometown of Winnipeg.

Upon reaching England, the cub became the mascot of the brigade, following the soldiers throughout their camp on the Salisbury Plain. When the brigade was called to France, however, Winnie could not continue on. Colebourn loaned his pet to the London Zoo, where she became a popular attraction. When the war ended, he returned and formally donated Winnie to the zoo.

It was there that Christopher Robin Milne became captivated by the animal, who gave children rides and ate the food they fed to him. When Christopher Robin's father, journalist A. A. Milne, wrote his classic children's story *Winnie-the-Pooh*, he named the main character after the bear his son was so fond of.

goods was also plummeting. Unemployment rose, and the Liberal government fell. The Conservative Party of Richard Bennett took over in August of 1930, just in time to feel the brunt of the down cycle.

Bennett did not experience much success in bringing Canada back. Droughts devastated the Prairie Provinces and wheat crops were destroyed. Unemployment reached record highs, and countless families were forced to go on relief. Dissatisfied with the lack of progress being made, Canadian voters made their feelings known at the polls. William Lyon Mackenzie King and the Liberal Party were returned to power in 1935.

WORLD WAR II

The effects of the depression lasted until the outbreak of World War II. Canada declared war on Germany on September 10, 1939, shortly after Britain did so. The difference of one week proclaimed to everyone Canada's right to make its own decisions.

Once again, thousands of Canadians volunteered for duty overseas. Remembering the problems the draft controversy had caused in World War I, King promised that this time there would be no conscription. The economy began its recovery as factories again turned out planes, ships, tanks, munitions, and other wartime supplies. Canadian farms increased wheat production for export abroad.

As in the First World War, however, casualties mounted, and the number of volunteers could not match the demand for replacements. Prime Minister King went to the people with a referendum asking to be released from his earlier promise. The majority of British Canadians voted in favor of the move, but once again French Canadians opposed it. The two segments of the population were driven further apart by this action when riots broke out in the province of Quebec. The potentially inflammatory situation was not defused until the war ended in 1945 and the draftees were quickly demobilized.

A PERIOD OF GROWTH

The decade following the end of the conflict was a period of reconstruction, ushering in the greatest growth cycle in the country's history. Factories switched over from manufacturing planes and ships to producing peacetime goods and supplies. Louis St. Laurent, who succeeded King as prime minister in 1948, ran the country like a business. Tens of thousands of Europeans emigrated from their homelands to start new lives in Canada's considerable expanses. The majority settled in the larger cities, which led to rapid urban growth. The discovery of oil and gas in the province of Alberta in 1947 also spurred the country's transformation from an agricultural nation into an industrial one. Foreign nations, particularly the United States, invested huge sums of money in Canadian industries.

With the economy now restored and production on the rise, the government turned its attention to internal reforms. Several social programs were instituted during the war, and others were initiated soon after. Among these were social security, unemployment compensation, veterans' benefits, and financial aid to families with young children. This increased concern for the well-being of the citizenry was a major reason why the economically distressed region of Newfoundland joined Canada as its tenth province in 1949.

Canada also continued to assert itself in postwar international politics. In 1947 it became one of the founding members of the United Nations. Two years later Canada joined the defense alliance known as the North Atlantic Treaty Organization (NATO), together with the United States and ten Western European countries.

PROBLEMS AT HOME

Not everyone, however, shared in Canada's new wealth. The Prairie and Atlantic Provinces did not enjoy as many of the benefits of the economic upsurge as did the more industrialized provinces, like Ontario and Quebec. In addition, part of the citizenry felt that St. Laurent was selling out to the Americans, as U.S. investments increased and the relationship between the two neighbors grew closer.

Together with U.S. president Harry Truman, St. Laurent helped lay the groundwork for an agreement between Canada and the United States to build the Saint Lawrence Seaway. Construction of the joint project was completed in 1959, allowing oceangoing vessels access to the Great Lakes for the first time.

It was another grandiose project—a planned 2,175-mile-long natural gas pipeline from Alberta to Montreal—that led to St. Laurent's eventual downfall. Opposition to the project enabled the Progressive Conservatives to upset the

Canadian troops fought alongside British and Allied soldiers during World War II. Canada considered implementing a draft when volunteers became scarce, however, the issue divided the nation between British proponents and French opponents.

Liberals in the 1957 election. Saskatchewan native John Diefenbaker became the first postwar prime minister raised west of Ontario.

Diefenbaker spoke out for the people and against big business. His term in office saw an increase in the incomes of farmers and fishermen in the Prairie and Maritime Provinces and continued expansion of the social welfare system. "I was criticized for being too much concerned with the average Canadians," he once said. "I can't help that; I am one of them!"

The Liberals returned to power in 1963 under the leadership of Lester Bowles Pearson. Pearson continued to improve medical and hospital insurance for Canadians and introduced the Canada Pension Plan, which provided a nationwide system of contributory pensions. His five years as prime minister were marked by a heightened sense of nationalism. In 1964 Canada adopted a new national flag. The old Red Ensign, which had served as Canada's flag since 1924, had graphically portrayed Canada's ties with England. The new flag featured a red maple leaf on a white background, bordered on both sides by vertical red panels.

As the decade progressed, however, a new set of problems came to the forefront. The economy sagged and unemploy-

The Saint Lawrence Seaway was completed in 1959. As a joint venture between Canada and the United States, the waterway finally allowed sea vessels to reach vital industrial ports on the Great Lakes.

Members of the House of Commons celebrate after the maple leaf flag is adopted in 1964. Canada's previous flag carried a symbolic representation of the country's link to England.

ment rose, in part due to the large number of American draft dodgers who entered the country in protest of U.S. involvement in Vietnam.

"MASTERS IN OUR HOUSE"

French Canadian frustrations also intensified. For the most part, Quebecers (or as they called themselves, Quebecois) had isolated themselves from English-speaking Canadians over the previous two hundred years, fearful of losing their identity and having their culture destroyed by being absorbed into the British mainstream. In so doing, French Canadians tended to remain in rural areas and to be less active in business, education, and health affairs than their English counterparts. Indeed, many English Canadians felt themselves to be superior to the French and looked down upon them as second-class citizens.

As Canada became industrialized, more and more Quebecers moved to the cities. The quiet revolution got underway as Quebec nationalism awakened from what became known as "the long night." Jean Lesage became leader of the Quebec provincial government in 1960, ushering in a wave of reform. Quebecois began to assert themselves, insisting on being *maîtres chez nous,* or "masters in our house." Several radical groups went even further, calling for independence for Quebec as a separate country.

Separatists rally around a French monument in Montreal in 1965. Although the government tried to cater to French requests by making Canada a bilingual nation, radical separatists urged secession from the anglicized portions of the country.

Prime Minister Pearson empathized with the Quebecers and encouraged them to become more involved in national politics. One of those who did so was Pierre Elliott Trudeau, who became prime minister upon Pearson's retirement in 1968.

Though popular, Trudeau's attempts to unify the country met with varying degrees of success. The Official Languages Act of 1969 made Canada a bilingual country. Government workers were required to learn French, road signs were posted in both languages, and television and radio stations were encouraged to begin broadcasting programs in French. The laws were aimed at undercutting the separatist movement but were only moderately successful. Extremist groups demanded more.

THE MOVEMENT WEAKENS

One such terrorist organization was the Front de la Libération du Québec. The FLQ conducted a series of bombings and in 1970 kidnapped and murdered Quebec labor minister Pierre Laporte. Prime Minister Trudeau, acting at the request of the Quebec government, responded by issuing the War Measures Act, which, in effect, imposed martial law in Canada. This meant that civil rights were suspended for a period of time while a state of possible insurrection existed. Members of the FLQ were rounded up, and guns and explosives were confiscated. The FLQ was eventually crushed, but the separatist movement survived.

In 1976 the separatist Parti Québecois won a majority of seats in Quebec's provincial legislature. Under the leadership of provincial prime minister René Lévesque, the PQ called for a 1980 referendum in Quebec to vote on the separatist issue. This proposal for "sovereignty-association" would have given the party leaders the power to negotiate for Quebec's independence. About 60 percent of the electorate voted to reject the proposal, however, feeling that separatism was costing them jobs. With the movement thus weakened, the Parti Québecois soon fell from power. Tensions were eased once again.

With the issue of Quebec's independence settled for the time being, Trudeau focused attention on his other goal of weakening Canadian ties to Britain. The result of these efforts was the 1981 Canadian Constitution and Charter of Rights and Freedoms, agreed upon by the federal and provincial governments, except that of Quebec. These reforms were enacted in the Constitution Act of 1982. No longer would changes in the constitution have to be approved in Britain. The last vestige of Canada's colonial status had been removed.

By the time Trudeau resigned in 1984, the Canadian economy had taken a turn for the worse. Unemployment had risen to its highest point since the depression. In an attempt to revitalize the economy, Prime Minister Brian Mulroney proposed the 1985 Free Trade Agreement (FTA) with the United States. This agreement called for most tariffs between the two countries to be dropped. There were spirited debates about the FTA in the Canadian Parliament, with some arguing that it would increase the country's dependence on its neighbor to the south. It was Mulroney's contention that since it would increase trade, it would also result in more jobs for Canadians. When the Progressive Conservatives won reelection in the 1988 elections, it indicated public approval for the agreement. The Canadian Parliament passed the FTA that December.

THE MEECH LAKE ACCORD

Another of Mulroney's goals was to win Quebec's approval of constitutional changes that the other provinces had accepted with the Constitution Act of 1982. A major stumbling block was Quebec's demand to be recognized as a "distinct society." This would have given Parliament and the provincial legislatures the role of preserving both the French-speaking and English-speaking character of Canada. Federal services, for example, would have to be provided in both official languages if there was "significant demand." Opponents were unwilling to approve any agreement that conferred special status to any province or people.

In April 1987 Mulroney gathered the nine provincial premiers and Quebec's prime minister (as Quebec's premier was

When tensions between the French Canadians and the national government prompted the resignation of the liberal prime minister, conservative candidate Kim Campbell (pictured) took office in 1993. Although her tenure was brief, she was the first woman to serve as prime minister.

called) together at his chalet at Meech Lake. There, he got them to approve an agreement known as the Meech Lake Accord, which, he said, "brought Quebec back into the constitution" by acceding to its demands. Mulroney hoped the agreement would end "Quebec's estrangement from the Canadian constitutional family, on terms that are good for Quebec, good for our other regions and good for Canada."

When the Quebec government passed measures that appeared to violate the rights of Anglophones [English speakers], such as prohibiting the use of English on outdoor commercial signs, public sentiment among the English-speaking population turned against Quebec. Meech Lake collapsed when the provincial governments of Newfoundland and Manitoba failed to ratify it by the June 22, 1990, deadline.

Prime Minister Mulroney continued his pursuit of an acceptable agreement with the Charlottetown Accord of 1992. This, too, was rejected, this time by six of the ten provinces.

Mulroney's approval rating had dropped precipitously, and in February of 1993 he announced his resignation after eight years in office. He was succeeded by Kim Campbell, who had been Canada's minister of defense. Upon taking office on June 25, Campbell became the first woman to serve as Canada's prime minister. Her tenure, however, was brief. The Conservative Party was soundly defeated in the October election, and the Liberals, under Jean Chrétien, came into power at the end of the year.

In September 1994, the separatist Parti Québecois returned to power in Quebec under the leadership of Jacques Parizeau. A 1995 referendum once again called for a vote on secession. Again, the proposal was turned down, but this time by only the narrowest of margins. Barely 50.6 percent of voters favored continued union with the rest of Canada. Shortly after the vote, Canada's Parliament passed a resolution recognizing Quebec's linguistic and cultural autonomy as a distinct society within Canada.

As the twenty-first century draws near, a solid core of French Canadians continue to feel that their interests are being ignored by the rest of Canada. The separatist movement remains a cloud hanging over the Canadian landscape.

A Nation of Diversity

Canada's closest friend and ally, the United States, has a population ten times larger, in a land 10 percent smaller than its neighbor to the north. Moreover, the vast majority of Canadians lives within two hundred miles of the thirty-four-hundred-mile-long Canadian-American border. These facts help explain why Americans have a hard time thinking of Canada as a "foreign" country. Most Canadians speak English, wear the same kind of clothes, eat the same foods, watch many of the same television programs, read many of the same magazines, and go about their daily lives in much the same way as do Americans.

With a country as large as Canada, however, it would be a mistake to think there are no differences, even within regions of the country itself. A fisherman in Nova Scotia, for example, will certainly have a different lifestyle than a wheat farmer in Saskatchewan; an Inuit child on the tundra of the north surely has little in common with a French youngster living in Quebec. Canada has different cultures and languages, a wide variety of geographical settings, and a style all its own.

Native Peoples

Canada's native peoples—classified as Indian, Inuit, and Métis—account for less than 2 percent of the nation's population. The half million Indians who are registered under the Indian Act of Canada consist of 633 different tribes, or First Nations, as they prefer to be called. The majority live on 2,250 largely self-governing reservations. A "registered," or status, Indian is recognized under federal law as being entitled to certain rights, benefits, and privileges. Among these are inclusion in all universal federal programs, such as Child Tax Benefit, Old Age Security, and Unemployment Insurance. Registered Indians are excluded from having to pay certain federal and provincial personal and real property taxes. Native people face

At Fort Qu'Applle, Saskatchewan, a young girl displays the pride Canadian Indians take in their cultural heritage.

a constant struggle against the perception that they are "inferior," or "non-people." Government intervention has attempted to bring improvements to their way of life, but these were not always successful. Until about a half century ago, mortality rates were high, the school system had failed, and housing standards on reserves were poor. It was not until the 1960s that significant improvements could be seen. Health standards were elevated, and life expectancy increased. By the 1970s Indians had procured full political and legal rights and are now represented in most sectors of the workforce. Unemployment remains high, however, and housing is still substandard in many regions. The federal government is continuing to work with native groups in an effort to improve social conditions on reservations.

Because of improved living conditions and medical attention, Indians are among the fastest growing ethnic groups in Canada today, in addition to being the oldest. Native groups that call Canada home include the Maliseet, Algonquian, Iroquois, Micmac, Huron, and Ojibwa in the eastern regions; the Blackfoot, Cree, and Assiniboin of the plains; the Kwakiutl, Bella Coola, and Haida of the Pacific coast; and the Déné, Tsimshian, and Slavey of the subarctic regions. Each community has its own traditions and language that it is reluctant to surrender.

In Manitoba and Alberta, communities of Métis live their existence of mixed native and French heritage. As descendants of French fur traders who married native women, the Métis have a religion, language and customs that are a blend of the two cultures.

INUIT

The Inuit are the native people who live in the arctic regions. Canada is home to approximately 25 percent of the world's Inuit population, most of whom live in small communities along the northern shores of Canada's mainland and in the arctic islands of the region. Until relatively recently, the Inuit were usually called by the Cree Indian name, Eskimo, which means "eater of raw meat." The natives themselves find the name derogatory, preferring instead Inuit, which they translate as "only people," fitting for the lone inhabitants of the frozen area.

For hundreds of years, the Inuit lived in almost total isolation. The fur trade and whaling industries eventually brought them into contact with Europeans. Hunting was central to the Inuit way of life and remains so to this day. Since World War II, the federal government has recognized the need for improved social services for the Inuit. Attempts have been made to move the small, scattered family groups into larger, more stable communities. Since these communities are located in remote areas, it has been difficult merging the Inuit into the general labor market.

Today Inuit members sit in both houses of Parliament and are well represented at the territorial ministerial level. Canada's Inuit have also joined those of Greenland, Alaska, and Russia in forming the Inuit Circumpolar Conference to address issues crucial to their lives.

Inuit children prepare to go on a hunting and fishing trip, essential activities that support their arctic lifestyle.

French-British Heritage

Aside from native peoples, the cultural groups with the longest continuous history in Canada are the French and English.

The lines were drawn between the French and English in Canada by the 1750s, as the animosities between the two motherlands carried over to the New World. From the time Britain forced France to surrender its holdings, the French in Quebec remained isolated and defeated. Regional affairs basically were a matter of a largely English-speaking government dictating to a mostly French-speaking populace.

Confederation gave more power to the provincial governments, but for the most part, the English remained the businessmen and power brokers, and the French, the farmers and workers; the English were Protestant, and the French, Roman Catholic; the English were the majority, and the French, the visible minority.

It was not until the 1950s that a significant change was noticed. The *révolution tranquille,* or the Quiet Revolution, was promoted by a group of art, literary, and political figures in order to strengthen the cultural fabric of French society. As the movement gained momentum, Quebecois began to take pride in their culture and became more protective of their identity. By the 1970s this "revolution" had evolved into the separatist movement. The Parti Québecois came into power, enacting legislation that caused resentment among English-speaking Canadians. Quebecois, more assertive and self-confident than in the past, began to take control over the province's internal affairs. For the first time, the rest of Canada recognized Quebec as a force that would have to be considered.

More than at any time in the past, French- and English-speaking communities are now equal partners. Communication between the two is necessary due to economic ties and political commitments. Culturally, however, the two societies share little in common. They continue to live their lives, as writer Hugh MacLennan has described it, of "two solitudes."

Other Immigrant Groups

Thousands of British Loyalists emigrated from the thirteen colonies during and after the American Revolution to express their allegiance to the British Crown. Since then, immigrants have been welcomed for the most part to Canadian shores.

Waves of Europeans crossed the Atlantic Ocean in the late 1800s, lured to the western plains by offers of free land. The next largest group, after the British and French, were the Germans. Today Germanic communities may be found in Ontario, the Prairie Provinces, and Nova Scotia. Of all the ethnic groups, Germans have perhaps most fully assimilated into the French and English communities. Italians, the next largest group, have generally settled in large cities, such as Toronto and Montreal. Ukrainians flocked to Canada, settling in Manitoba, Saskatchewan, and Alberta, where the prairies resemble the steppes of their homeland. Russians, Romanians, Belgians, Scandinavians, Austrians, and other Europeans also came to the western regions.

Chinatown in Vancouver, British Columbia, is a busy metropolis for Canada's Asian population.

ASIAN CANADIANS

The Chinese first arrived in Canada to work in the gold mines during the Fraser River gold rush. When construction began on the Canadian Pacific Railway, Chinese laborers played an important role in performing the dangerous work. The difficulties of building through the rugged expanse of land were staggering, as tunnels had to be dug through mountains and bridges built over rivers. It was estimated that one Chinese worker died for every railroad tie laid. Today Canada's Asian community is centered on the west coast, where it comprises 3 percent of the population of British Columbia.

Liberalized immigration policies in the 1960s opened the doors to thousands of others from Third World nations. Asians, Indians, Arabs, Hispanics, and Caribbean blacks have immigrated to the Dominion, adding their cultural inflections to the mix. Most of these groups have remained in their own urban enclaves or self-contained agricultural communities, each adding another tile to the Canadian mosaic.

In 1971 Canada established a national official government policy of multiculturalism. In pursuit of its goal of eliminating discrimination, a series of developments over the past quarter century have been implemented. Among these were the appointment of a minister of state for multiculturalism in 1972, the enactment of the Canadian Human Rights Act in 1977, and the passage of employment equity legislation in 1986. In addition to these federal initiatives, the provincial governments have established their own programs and guidelines.

AFRICAN CANADIANS

The first Africans in Canada came to New France in 1628, brought over from Africa to work as slaves in French Canadian households. Slavery was not abolished until more than two hundred years later, by the British Emancipation Act of 1833. Blacks still suffered discrimination even after emancipation, often being confined to ghettos in the larger cities.

By the mid–nineteenth century, many blacks were immigrating to Canada to escape the brutality and oppression they suffered as slaves in the southern part of the United States. The secret network of people and places that enabled them to reach a haven in the North was known as the Underground Railroad. The network got its name from the use of railway terms to refer to its various parts. Routes that were used were known as "lines," hiding places along the way as "stations," and those who helped the slaves reach freedom as "conductors."

Between 1840 and 1860, hundreds of former slaves managed to make their way to Canada. The spiritual "Follow the Drinking Gourd" gave the slaves hidden advice to keep their eyes on the Gourd, or the Big Dipper, in the sky. The Gourd pointed the way north to "heaven," or Canada.

In recent times, many blacks have emigrated from Africa and the Caribbean region, often without speaking any English. They still face discrimination to an extent, which has made it even harder for them to be absorbed into the fabric of Canadian life. Racial prejudice, unfortunately, has not been completely eliminated.

FAMILY AND HOME LIFE

Once, small communities dominated Canadian life. Today approximately 90 percent of the nation's people are clustered on just 12 percent of the land, mostly within 200 miles of the American border. A further breakdown shows approximately three-quarters of the populace living in the lowlands of the east, and only one-quarter in the more rugged west.

Following the end of World War II, there was a major change in Canada's population distribution. Thousands of immigrants arrived, mainly settling in the cities. More and more Canadians joined them, and the nation became predominantly urbanized almost overnight. Today, only 24 percent of the Canadian population lives in rural areas, and only 3 percent of the total labor force make their living by farming. In the rural areas, small villages and towns remain the center of social activity.

Life in Canadian cities is similar to that in large cities in any other industrialized nation of the world. Tall apartment buildings dot the landscape and are home to hundreds of families. With less living area per person, city dwellers in Canada face many of the same obstacles that confront their counterparts elsewhere. For the most part, however, problems such as crime, homelessness, prostitution, and illegal drug dealing are not as formidable. This could change in the future, as reductions in government spending for social services may lead to increased frustrations. In addition,

City dwellers in Canada often live in high-rise apartment complexes like these dwellings in Toronto.

increased racial tension has been an unfortunate by-product of a more lenient immigration policy. On the whole, however, visitors to Canadian cities are impressed by their cleanliness, safety, and overall appearance.

LIFE IN THE ARCTIC

The majority of those who live in the arctic wilderness of the frozen north are Indians and Inuit. Many of these native Canadians prefer their "primitive" lifestyles and resist attempts to assimilate them into the "modern" world. Indians can still be found on reserves, where poverty is the rule and alcoholism abounds. Inuit struggle to preserve their nomadic existence, often resisting government efforts to relocate them to more established settlements. Although much of their traditional culture has been destroyed, native peoples are rediscovering their heritage and fighting for the right to be recognized as distinct societies. The problem of native alienation in the "white man's world" remains a delicate one as the century nears its end.

WHEN CULTURES CLASH

A tragic example of the repercussions when two cultures clash occurred at Davis Inlet, off the coast of Labrador, in early 1993.

In 1967 a community of 530 Mushuau Innu ("people of the barrens") were moved from their traditional home on the mainland to a small island in Davis Inlet. The government hoped that the Innu, who had been nomadic caribou hunters for thousands of years, would be able to establish a fishing industry in their new home. Promises of better housing, sewage systems, and running water failed to materialize, however, although families were supplied with other amenities of modern life, such as cable television and snowmobiles.

Unfortunately, the undertaking also introduced the nomadic society to some of the undesirable features of the twentieth century as well—alcoholism, unemployment, poverty, violence, child abuse, drug addiction, and suicide among them.

In January 1993, six twelve- and fourteen-year-old Innu children were found in a shed, after trying to kill themselves by inhaling gasoline fumes. When discovered, the youngsters fought off attempts to save them, saying they wanted to die. Exactly one year earlier, six of their friends had died in a fire while their parents were out drinking. The world soon learned that nearly one person of four in the community had tried to commit suicide in the previous year.

The Innu have asked to be relocated to a site on the mainland eleven miles away. Wishing to avoid another failed relocation, the government is proceeding with caution.

Although Canada is the second-largest country in the world in terms of area, nearly 90 percent of its land has no permanent population. More than 75 percent of its inhabitants can be found living in large metropolitan areas.

Toronto is Canada's largest and fastest-growing city, lying on the shores of Lake Ontario with a population of more than four million. Sometimes called "New York without the dirt," it is unquestionably the business, financial, and cultural heart of the country today. Known as York when it was founded in 1792, Toronto's location on a natural harbor made it a center of trade and transportation for Canada. The city's modern downtown skyline boasts the world's tallest freestanding building, the Canadian National Tower. As a major cultural center, it offers the Toronto Symphony Orchestra, the National Ballet of Canada, the Canadian Opera Company, and several museums and art galleries. Although Toronto has gained status as a first-rate modern metropolis, with its prominent steel and glass skyscrapers and sprawling underground shopping malls, it has also retained much of its charm with a wide mixture of lively ethnic neighborhoods. The city, arguably the most ethnically diverse in the Confederation, is rated one of the world's top ten cities to live in.

Canada is home to 25 percent of the world's Inuit population. This Inuit hunter might be better recognized by some as an Eskimo, the name Cree Indians gave to these native people.

FRENCH CANADIAN CULTURE

With more than three million inhabitants, Montreal is the second-largest French-speaking city in the world, trailing only Paris in size. It was founded in 1642 by Jesuit missionaries and quickly became a fur trading center. Montreal dominates the economic and cultural life in the province of Quebec. It developed into an important port and industrial center when the Lachine Canal opened the Saint Lawrence River and the Great Lakes to oceangoing ships. The city is a center of French Canadian culture, as two-thirds of its inhabitants are of French descent. Many Quebecers migrated

The Canadian National Tower, the world's tallest free-standing building, is a popular tourist attraction in Toronto.

to the city with the onset of the Quiet Revolution of the 1960s and 1970s, causing many English-speaking inhabitants and businesses to leave. The result was a loss of status as Canada's major city, with it being overtaken by Toronto. Although it gives an outward appearance of a modern city, Montreal still retains many old neighborhoods, which give it an old-world charm. The city was the site of Expo 67, the world's fair that marked Canada's centennial. It also hosted the 1976 Summer Olympics.

In addition to being Canada's third-largest city, Vancouver is also its busiest seaport, nestled between the Pacific coast and the Coast Mountains. It is the burgeoning financial center of western Canada, located some three thousand miles west of Montreal. Looking out west over the Pacific, Vancouver's rapid rate of growth can be partially attributed to its many investors from the Far East. This is easier to understand when taking into account the fact that the city is some 350 miles closer to Tokyo, Japan, than to Halifax, Nova Scotia. The Asian culture flourishes in the city's Chinatown neighborhood— the second-largest one in North America, after that of San Francisco. Established in 1885, Vancouver grew rapidly as a terminus of the Canadian Pacific Railway. The numerous parks that dot the city, taken together with its location near the Coast Mountains, make Vancouver one of the most picturesque cities in North America and the shining star of Canada's west coast.

OTTAWA AND OTHER MAJOR CITIES

Ottawa is the capital city of Canada and, along with its sister city of Hull, the country's fourth-largest urban center. When the city was named capital of the British province of Canada by Queen Victoria, it was known as Bytown. At the time, it was a curious choice for a capital since it was a logging settlement in the center of the lumbering region. Supposedly, it was chosen because it was on the boundary separating English and French Canada, and because it was a "safe" distance from the United States, in case the Americans ever decided to invade their neighbor to the north. The city was renamed Ottawa and chosen as the national capital upon Confederation in 1867. In addition to being the hub of government activities, Ottawa is also a center for tourism. The National Arts Centre and the National Gallery are both located in Ontario's second-largest city, a hundred miles southwest of Montreal. A favorite Ottawa attraction is the Rideau Canal, which winds through the heart of the city. In winter, the canal becomes the world's longest skating rink.

The most northerly metropolis in Canada, Edmonton is the provincial capital of Alberta. It is responsible for turning out 10 percent of Canada's petrochemical products. This modern municipality is home to Canada's largest theater— the Citadel Theatre—and the nation's largest planetarium. Its greatest tourist attraction, however, is the West Edmonton

Traditional events, such as this parade in Vancouver's Chinatown, attract tourists to Canada's cities every year.

Mall. Home to more than eight hundred stores, one hundred restaurants, and the world's largest indoor amusement park, the mall is North America's largest. Many visitors stay at one of its hotels and spend their entire vacation without ever setting foot outside. The city celebrates its heritage with a series of observances during the year. Because of this, Edmonton is often called Canada's Festival City.

Located in the foothills of the Canadian Rockies, Calgary is the center of Canada's petroleum industry. The city was founded in 1875 by the North-West Mounted Police. The fort that they built was named after Calgary Bay in Scotland. The late 1940s signaled the start of an unprecedented boom period, as large reserves of oil were discovered in the region. Almost overnight Calgary became a major metropolis. Thousands of Americans flocked to the region. At present, they constitute approximately 20 percent of the town's population. The city is home to the Calgary Stampede, the most famous rodeo in the world. Calgary received worldwide attention in 1988 when it hosted the Winter Olympics.

Quebec City is Canada's oldest city and the focal point of French Canadian culture and tradition. First settled in 1608, it

The Rideau Canal winds its way through Ottawa, the seat of Canada's government.

is located high atop a bluff on the northern bank of the Saint Lawrence River. In
addition to being a fur trading center,
Quebec City was also the religious center of the region, with the Roman
Catholic Church of New France established there in 1659. Quebec City is important historically as the site of the
battle that ultimately decided the war
between France and Britain for control
of Canada. With this as its legacy, the city
has become the home of the Quebecois
separatist movement. As the provincial
capital, Quebec City embodies the
province's motto, *Je me souviens* (I re-
member). Quebecois tradition and culture can be seen at every turn. The Old
City area is the only walled city in North
America, surrounded by restored fortifi-
cations. Many old buildings have been
preserved in this part of the city, including the star-shaped
fortress known as the Citadelle. Modern Quebec City, lying outside the walls, contains all the earmarks of a modern major metropolis, including high-rise buildings and shopping malls.

*Another popular
Canadian tourist draw
is the Calgary
Stampede, the most
well-known rodeo in
the world.*

WINNIPEG

Winnipeg is the provincial capital of Manitoba and home to
more than half of the province's inhabitants. The historic hub
of the fur trade in days gone by, the city boasts the greatest
cultural diversity in the Prairie Provinces. Thousands of European immigrants entered the region upon the completion
of the Canadian Pacific Railway in 1885. The Ukrainian Canadian population is particularly prominent in Winnipeg, and
the French Quarter of Saint Boniface is the largest French
Canadian community west of Quebec.

Founded in 1749, Halifax is the largest city in the Atlantic
Provinces. Its status as an important shipping and fishing center is due to its deepwater harbors. Halifax was a center of the
shipbuilding industry when it suffered a devastating tragedy
in 1917. A supply ship carrying twenty-five hundred tons of explosives collided with another boat in the harbor, and the resulting explosion leveled part of the city. Approximately two

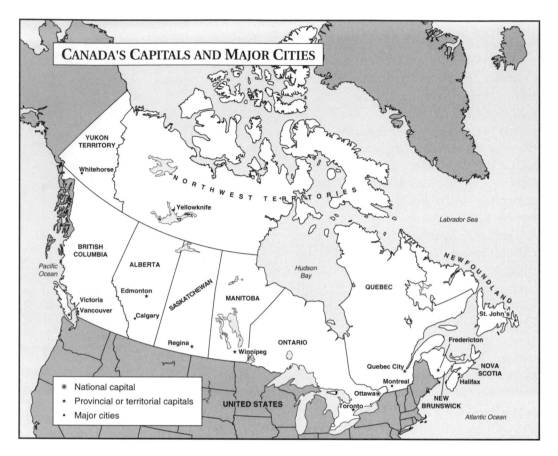

CANADA'S CAPITALS AND MAJOR CITIES

- ⊛ National capital
- ★ Provincial or territorial capitals
- • Major cities

thousand people died and another two thousand were injured. It was the largest man-made explosion of any kind until the first atomic bomb was detonated in 1945. Following reconstruction, the city resumed its standing as an important commercial port.

ELEMENTARY AND SECONDARY EDUCATION

As provided by the British North America Act, public education in Canada is under the jurisdiction of each individual province. The major exception concerns Indian and Inuit children, who are taught in schools run by the federal government. Children in these schools learn about their native heritage, as well as the more traditional subjects. The government also controls education in the Yukon and Northwest Territories. The federal government has an indirect involvement by providing financial support for postsecondary education through the Canada Student Loans Program.

Public education is free through secondary school. In Quebec, it is extended to include *collèges d'enseignement général et professionnel* (colleges of general and professional instruction—CEGEP). More than $54 billion was spent on education in Canada in 1993, or 8 percent of the country's gross domestic product. That rate is among the highest in the world among industrialized nations.

Children usually begin kindergarten at age five or six and attend elementary school through the eighth grade. They take traditional subjects such as math, social studies, science, and reading. Afterward, they move on to four years of high school where, in addition to the standard academic subjects, they may select courses that will prepare them for either university, community college, or the workplace. In Quebec, CEGEPs must be attended for two to three years to prepare for the university or a specific career. Private parochial schools—sometimes called "separate" schools—are available to children of different religious denominations in some provinces.

A relatively recent innovation is the development of French-immersion schools in Quebec. In these schools, English-speaking children have some, or all, of their courses taught entirely in French. The programs vary from school to school, but in most cases the children study exclusively in French for two to four years. About half of their remaining courses are in French for as long as they remain in the program. This time also varies, as students may begin immersion courses as early as kindergarten, or as late as sixth or seventh grade. The success of the program is one of the reasons why Quebec has the highest percentage of bilingual citizens of any province.

POSTSECONDARY EDUCATION

Until the 1960s, most postsecondary education was through private institutions with a religious affiliation. With the rising demand, however, systems of publicly operated institutions have developed. The percentage of high school students who go on to postsecondary schools is currently about 40 percent, and more than 55 percent are female. There are more than seventy universities in Canada, almost all financially dependent on the provincial governments and most offering instruction in English rather than French. The most prestigious institutions include Queen's University, the University of Toronto ("Harvard of the North"), McGill University, the Université de Montreal, and Laval University, which is the oldest university in the nation. Tuition costs are far below those at comparable schools in the United States.

RELIGION

The three major churches in Canada are the Roman Catholic, the United Church of Canada, and the Anglican. Roman Catholics constitute just less than half the population and the great majority of the French-speaking segment. In 1925 the United Church of Canada was established, uniting the Methodist Church, the Congregationalist Church, and most of the Presbyterians under one designation. Today they comprise approximately 15 percent of the citizenry. The Anglican Church lays claim to another 10 percent, while the remainder follow the beliefs of other Protestant denominations, Eastern Orthodoxy, Judaism, Hinduism, Islam, Buddhism, and various other smaller sects.

Students play football at McGill University in Montreal. McGill is one of Canada's most prestigious learning institutions.

Though church and state are separate in Canada, the state does provide support to various religious institutions, particularly schools.

St. Paul's church in Trinity Bay, Newfoundland. Though various forms of Christianity remain as Canada's dominant religions, the country's diverse populations have spread a host of other beliefs throughout the nation.

SOCIAL SERVICES

Canada's federal and provincial governments provide for an extensive range of health and social service programs. These programs are based on the principle of universality. Anyone may receive benefits, regardless of a person's wealth or income status.

National health insurance benefits cover virtually all doctor bills and hospital costs. Treatment is dispensed according to need, not the ability of a person to pay. The program has been extremely successful but is also quite expensive. With health costs soaring, there has been a call for fundamental changes in the system. Canadians, however, are reluctant to tamper with a system that has helped them maintain one of the highest life-expectancy levels (74.7 for males and 81.7 for females, born in 1994) in the world.

PUBLIC WELFARE PROGRAMS

Other national programs, in addition to health care, include those that provide family aid, pensions, unemployment and disability insurance, child benefits, maternity benefits, and subsidized housing. Interest in many of these was stimulated by the depression of the 1930s. Plans to redistribute the country's wealth to benefit the less well-to-do members of society were formulated and put into effect shortly afterward. Today families with children can claim payments

Canada transformed from a primarily agricultural economy into an industrialized nation during the twentieth century. It now supports a variety of manufacturers, including this combined paper, pulp, and lumber mill in British Columbia.

under the Family Allowances Act, while all Canadians can look forward to receiving a government pension when they are ready to retire.

The shift in emphasis in the structure of Canada's economy since the turn of the century has been dramatic. Prior to 1900, the majority of Canadians earned their livings in the farming, mining, forestry, and fishing industries. All that has changed in the last one hundred years. Today Canada is one of the leading industrialized nations in the entire world. Less than one person in ten continues to labor in the aforementioned fields.

The service industry—the fastest growing sector—now accounts for almost 75 percent of Canadian jobs. This category includes those employed by banks, insurance companies, hospitals, schools, and restaurants, as well as those involved in transportation, communication, and recreation.

Manufacturing encompasses another 15 percent of the economy and is centered in the provinces of Quebec and Ontario. Canada leads all nations of the world in the production of newsprint and ranks high in food processing, paper production, and manufacturing transportation equipment. Other essentials in an industrialized society, such as electronic equipment, steel, and automobiles, are also produced in abundance.

Forest products, such as timber and paper, are Canada's single largest export, with a major share going to the United States. It is the third-largest producer of such products and the number-one exporter. Unfortunately, industrialization has its negative effects. Trees are being felled faster than they can be replenished. The threat to the country's forests from acid rain is a very real one and the issue of an ongoing dialogue between Canada and the United States.

Most of Canada's agriculture industry is centered in the Prairie Provinces, where the production of wheat is a top priority. Canada exports more wheat than any other country in the world, save for the United States. The Saint Lawrence lowlands area is the country's other main farming region, producing dairy products, fruits, and vegetables. Although the number of people employed in agriculture has decreased, farms have become larger. Improved technology has enabled farmers to meet the needs of a growing population. Prospects for the future are a cause for concern in some minds, however, as a percentage of land is lost each year due to development.

Much of the economy of the east and west coasts is still dependent on fishing. Canada remains the world's leading exporter of fish and fish products, transporting nearly 80 percent of its total production. The seas off Newfoundland continue to provide a wide array of seafood for fishermen in the Atlantic Provinces, while salmon are found in abundance in Pacific waters. As with forestry and agriculture, there is cause for concern for the future of the fisheries. The threat of foreign boats depleting the waters of their riches has given rise to talk of limiting foreign access to the region.

LEISURE

Canadians have a passion for sports and the outdoors. Most take advantage of the opportunities offered by their beautiful homeland whenever they can. Canada has an extensive park system, with twenty-eight national parks and over seven hundred national historic parks and sites to choose from. Among the more famous national parks are Banff and Jasper in Alberta; Glacier and Kootenai in British Columbia;

Riding Mountain in Manitoba; Fundy in New Brunswick; Cape Breton Highlands in Nova Scotia; Point Pelee and Pukaskwa in Ontario; Grasslands and Prince Albert in Saskatchewan; Wood Buffalo in the Northwest Territories; and Kluane in the Yukon.

Skiing, ice-skating, sledding, and snowmobiling are popular winter activities. Canada is home to hundreds of ski areas, including world-famous resorts at Banff, Alberta, and Whistler, British Columbia. A network of figure-skating clubs has helped the country produce gold-medal winners in both World Championship and Olympic competition. A new sport that has recently become popular is ringette. It is similar to hockey and is played mostly by women.

BLUENOSE

Occasionally, work and play come together in unusual ways. Such was the case in 1919 when a group of Nova Scotia schoonermen read a newspaper account of the America's Cup race that the New York Yacht Club had canceled due to twenty-three-mile-an-hour winds. Real seamen, they ventured, would laugh in the face of such "gales." The article inspired Senator William B. Smith, editor of the paper, to establish "The *Halifax Herald* North Atlantic Fisherman's International Competition" for bona fide working schooners of the United States and Canada.

After a series of elimination races was held in both countries, the final race for the International Fisherman's Trophy was won by the schooner *Esperanto,* out of Gloucester, Massachusetts. The disappointed Nova Scotians hired William Roue to design a ship that could challenge for the trophy in the future. The result was the schooner *Bluenose* (named after the traditional nickname for Nova Scotians), which was launched in 1921. Following a season of work in the fishery, as required by the rules, *Bluenose* went on to defeat Gloucester's *Elsie* to bring the trophy to Nova Scotia and become a national symbol of Canadian maritime spirit.

Over the succeeding two decades, *Bluenose* would not surrender the trophy in four further competitions. The ship's final moment of glory came in 1938 as she defeated the *Gertrude L. Thebaud,* with an average speed for the course of 14.15 knots. In the history of sailing, no canvased vessel had ever recorded a faster pace over a fixed course.

When lack of money caused her owner to sell her, the *Bluenose* spent her final years carrying freight in the Caribbean. She sank after striking a reef in the waters off Haiti in 1946. Her memory has been kept alive, however, as her image has graced the Canadian dime since 1937. In 1963 *Bluenose II* was launched as a reminder of the greatest schooner of all time.

Leisure activities in Canada include many winter sports such as skiing. Home to such well-known ski resorts as Banff and Whistler, Canada's slopes are popular among enthusiasts.

When the weather warms up, swimming, cycling, tennis, golf, windsurfing, rowing, track and field, and boating move to the forefront, while hunting, hiking, and camping are activities engaged in year-round.

Millions of Canadians of all ages participate in the four major team sports of baseball, basketball, football, and hockey. Hockey is without a doubt first in Canadian hearts, with organized leagues existing for youngsters who are not yet old enough to tie their own skates. Softball, soccer, and volleyball are also on the upswing.

Canadians recognize the contribution sports can make to the well-being of the individual and the community. Participation in international competitions helps Canada find a common ground on which to meet with others of differing cultural, political, and religious preferences.

4

THE CULTURE OF CANADA

When discussing Canadian culture, it is natural to dwell on the English and French components. In addition, with so large and influential a neighbor as the United States to the south, it is not surprising to also find a significant American component in the mix. In the early years of Canada's history, the arts generally took a backseat to less "trivial" pursuits. There was little time for the expression of artistic creativity when there were fields to be plowed, homes to be protected, and families to be raised in what could often be a hostile environment. Those artists and writers of the 1800s who did pursue their muse most often found their inspiration in French, English, and American traditions. It was not until the twentieth century that distinctly Canadian styles began to emerge.

In recent times Canadians have become more aware of the importance of maintaining their own distinct culture. The government gave a great boost to this movement when it established the Canada Council in 1957 for the purpose of promoting the arts. Since then, the council's budget has grown to nearly $100 million in support of Canadian endeavors in the arts and humanities. Local artists and performers no longer need look to Europe and America for inspiration. Canadians of diverse backgrounds are making important contributions in the fields of art, literature, music, and theater. The cultural diversity that is Canada is beginning to reveal itself to the rest of the world.

CHRISTIAN HOLIDAYS

Canadians celebrate their heritage by observing holidays and festivals throughout the year. The two most important for most Christian Canadians are Christmas and Easter.

When Christmas is celebrated on December 25, different groups commemorate it in different ways. Traditional meals are served and legends retold. While English children keep on the lookout for a sleigh pulled by eight reindeer, Dutch youngsters watch for one pulled by the eight-legged Sleipner, and Inuit children in the north look for one pulled by cows and horses. Whatever the culture, Christmas is a time for gift giving and family get-togethers. In most of Canada, the day following Christmas is celebrated as Boxing Day. It marks the traditional British day for opening church alms boxes and distributing the contents to the poor. Gifts to household employees and other service workers are also traditionally given on this day.

Easter is a time for reflection and going to church. Christ's rising from the dead is celebrated, and the beginning of spring noted. As in the United States, decorating eggs is a favorite activity with kids of all ages.

NATIONAL HOLIDAYS

Other Canadian national holidays familiar to Americans include New Year's Day, Labour Day, and Thanksgiving, although the last is celebrated for a different reason and on a different date. Remembrance Day in November corresponds to Veterans Day in the United States.

Victoria Day is the country's oldest national holiday, honoring the birthday of Queen Victoria of England on May 24. French-speaking Canadians in Quebec, however, have no desire to glorify the former British ruler. They call the holiday Dollard Day, honoring the seventeenth-century French soldier Dollard des Ormeaux, who lost his life while defending Montreal against the Iroquois Indians.

The Canadian equivalent of July 4th, celebrated three days earlier, is Canada Day, formerly called Dominion Day. This most important holiday is the birthday of the Confederation, which was formed by the British North America Act in 1867. Fireworks displays and picnics play a large part in the celebration.

An entrepreneur displays his Parliament Hill hat during Canada Day celebrations. Canada Day marks the birth of the Confederation that later developed into nationhood.

Other holidays are celebrated by different religious and ethnic groups, such as Yom Kippur by those of the Jewish faith, Burns' Night by Scots, Chinese New Year by Chinese, and Peter's Day by Russian Doukhobors. Other holidays are recognized in different provinces, such as Saint Jean Baptiste Day, Epiphany, Ash Wednesday, and Ascension Day in Quebec; Saint George's Day and Saint Patrick's Day in Newfoundland; and Discovery Day in the Yukon.

In addition to the various holidays, there are numerous festivals that take place throughout the year in different parts of the country. Among these are Oktoberfest in Kitchener and Waterloo, the Quebec Winter Carnival in Quebec City, Loyalist Days in Saint John, the Mummer's Day Parade in Newfoundland, the International Caravan in Toronto, the Tulip Festival in Ottawa, the Acadian Festival in Caraquet, Canada's National Ukrainian Festival in Dauphin, the Calgary Stampede in Calgary, Klondike Days in Edmonton, the Caribou Carnival in Yellowknife, and the Yukon Sourdough Rendezvous in Whitehorse.

ART

Painting is arguably the visual art most successful in expressing a distinct Canadian national identity. Toward the end of the seventeenth century, French-born clerics, such as Frère Luc, were the first Quebec painters. Following the British conquest, Thomas Davies, Joseph Légaré, Cornelius Krieghoff, and Paul Kane established reputations as being among the elite artists of the day, the first two through their landscapes, Krieghoff with his portrayals of settler life, and Kane in his paintings of Native peoples.

Canada's first nationalist school of painting was the work of the Group of Seven in the first quarter of the twentieth century. The group originally consisted of Franklin Carmichael, Lawren Harris, Alexander Young Jackson, Franz Johnston, Arthur Lismer, James Edward Hervey MacDonald, and Frederick Horsman Varley. An eighth man—Tom Thomson—was an inspiration for the group in its early years, but he died tragically in 1917, three years before they had their first showing as a group. The circle broke with the traditional school of realism popular at the time by boldly painting landscapes with vibrant colors, touched with a hint of the mysterious. At first their work met with a great deal of criticism. Gradually, however, they received critical acclaim in England and acceptance at home. The group disbanded in 1931 following their final exhibition at the Art Gallery of Toronto (now, the Art Gallery of Ontario), where many of their works are on permanent display.

Later Canadian artists of distinction, such as Emily Carr, David Milne, Jean-Paul Riopelle, Harold Town, and Jean-Paul Lemieux owe a debt of gratitude to the Group of Seven for taking the steps that made their later work possible.

Not all Canadian painters followed the Group of Seven. The *automatiste* movement in Montreal developed a dedicated following for their surrealistic works, which were influenced by Matisse and Picasso. One of these men—French Canadian Paul-Émile Borduas—attacked the government and advocated artistic and creative freedom in the 1948 declaration of his principles, *Refus Global*. His manifesto and paintings represent a significant milestone in Canadian art, having a positive influence on every creative calling. Fourteen artists of the day signed his manifesto, which proclaimed: "Let there be room for magic, room for hope, room for imaginativeness."

An artist sketches urban scenery in Quebec. From Paul Kane's realistic depictions of native people to the surrealism of Paul-Émile Borduas, Canada is the home to a legacy of diverse painting styles.

The period that followed was a boom time for art, as the number of galleries and exhibitions increased dramatically. The 1960s saw a style that favored geometrical abstraction introduced by Canadians Yves Gaucher, Guido Molinari, and Claude Tousignant. Most recently, a wide range of interests have been exhibited by a new generation of artists. Major names of today include Alexander Colville in the Atlantic region, and Jack Shadbolt, Toni Onley, and Gordon Smith in the west.

Sculpture and handicrafts of various types have played a less significant role in the Canadian artistic universe, with Robert Murray and David Rabinovitch among the internationally known. Interest in Inuit ivory and stone carvings and Indian totem pole carvings has increased of late. Haida sculptor Robert Davidson has established a reputation for himself as a native artist whose primitive themes are expressed in wood carvings and bronze sculptures.

A view of Simon Fraser University. The architecture was designed by Arthur Erickson, one of Canada's most respected architects.

ARCHITECTURE

Examples of the Georgian and Neoclassic styles of architecture popular in the eighteenth and nineteenth centuries can

still be found in the Dominion, as can the Italianate, Beaux Arts, and more recent styles. A closer examination also reveals a rather diverse range of modern styles.

Buildings designed to integrate with the environment are the hallmark of Arthur Erickson, one of Canada's most influential architects. His work includes Simon Fraser University in Burnaby, and Lethbridge University in southern Alberta. Other modern architects of note include Geoffrey Massey, Ron Thom, I. M. Pei, Raymond Moriyama, John C. Parkin, and Moshe Safdie.

Some of the more interesting modern structures of the Dominion may be found in Toronto. The CN Tower is the tallest freestanding structure in the world, stretching 1,815 feet above the city. The nearby SkyDome is the home of the Toronto Blue Jays and the world's first retractable domed sports stadium. The two curved buildings that make up Toronto's City Hall stand out in contrast to the rectangular skyscrapers of the neighborhood. The Ontario Science Centre in the Don Valley is another attraction not to be missed.

The curved buildings of Toronto's City Hall are an example of the innovative architecture that exists in that city.

Other examples of notable Canadian architecture include: Place Ville Marie in Montreal, which pioneered the concept of the shopping mall in 1962; the West Edmonton Mall, which is the largest shopping center in the world; the National Gallery of Canada in Ottawa, with its glass walls and high ceilings; and Habitat in Montreal, which was built as a modular residential building for Expo 67.

LITERATURE

Canadian literature may be separated into two basic branches: works written in French and works written in English. In many ways, the two have developed along similar paths, both mirroring Canadian history and life.

The earliest works were narratives or journals penned by explorers and settlers. A notable example is Marc Lescarbot's

Histoire de la Nouvelle France (1609). The first Canadian novel is considered to be the four-volume *History of Emily Montague* (1769) by Frances Brooke. Except for the volumes of a few authors like John Richardson and T. C. Haliburton, little of note was written before 1867.

Following Confederation, the first works of a truly Canadian nature began to appear. Canadian history became a topic of choice for poets and authors, and works such as "La Découverte du Mississippi" (1873) by Louis Honoré Fréchette and *The Golden Dog* (1877) by William Kirby saw the light of day. Just prior to World War I, the "poets of the Confederation" published poetry and fiction that became well known for blending realism and regionalism. Charles G. D. Roberts was arguably the most important member of this group. Émile Nelligan is often cited as the first major French Canadian poet. One of the most famous novels of the time is Lucy Maud Montgomery's *Anne of Green Gables* (1908), which paints a picture of life on Prince Edward Island.

Canadian literature has continued along a similar path in modern times. An important volume is Hugh MacLennan's *Two Solitudes* (1945), which examines the parallel French and English communities in Canada and helps one to understand the basis for the separatist movement. French Canada's contributions have come from the pens of Marie Claire Blais, Anne Hébert, Gabrielle Roy, Pierre Berton, and Jacques Godbout, among others. In 1978 Antonine Maillet won France's Prix Goncourt—the highest honor ever won by a Canadian author—for her novel of Acadia, *Pelagie's Return to the Homeland.* Brian Moore, Margaret Atwood, Alice Munro, Robertson Davies, Mordecai Richler, Saul Bellow, Will Durant, Jack Kerouac, Arthur Hailey, and Dorothy Livesay are among the best-known present-day English Canadian authors.

Today, publishing in Canada is giving more and more writers outlets for their work. Publishing houses can be found in every province, as can numerous literary magazines and journals. Canadian writers have also been encouraged through the formation of the League of Canadian Poets (1966) and the Writers' Union of Canada (1973).

SYMPHONIES AND OPERAS

The upsurge that has taken place in Canadian music since the 1940s had its foundation laid much earlier in the century.

The first civic symphony orchestra—L'Orchestre Symphonique de Quebec—was founded at the turn of the century. Today most major cities have their own symphonies, with the Montreal Symphony Orchestra, the National Arts Centre Orchestra, the Toronto Symphony Orchestra, and the Vancouver Symphony Orchestra the best known. Choral societies can also be found in most cities and towns.

Opera has not developed quite as rapidly in the Dominion. The Canadian Opera Company tours the country, but only the major cities have regular seasons. This is also a reflection on the dearth of good Canadian operas. *The Night Blooming Cereus* from James Reaney and John Beckwith is a prominent exception.

The lack of original Canadian classical music has not hindered Canadian-born performers from establishing reputations for themselves. Pianist Glenn Gould and singers Jon Vickers, Maureen Forrester, Lois Marshall, and Louis and Gino Quilico are recognized for their talents far beyond Canadian borders.

JAZZ AND POP

Jazz has also had a special place in Canadian hearts, with special thanks owed to Montreal's world-famous International Jazz Festival, which is held each summer. Pianist Oscar Peterson is an all-time great, while Ed Bickert, Lorraine Desmarais, Michel Donato, and Karen Young are up-and-coming performers held in high regard.

The popular music scene has received much more attention. Canadian performers like Neil Young, Joni Mitchell, Paul Anka, Leonard Cohen, Gordon Lightfoot, Buffy Sainte-Marie, Anne Murray, k.d. lang, Shania Twain, Alanis Morissette, and Céline Dion are known throughout the world. Roch Voisine and Daniel Lavoie are favorites with francophone (French-speaking)

Alanis Morissette receives a 1996 Grammy Award. She is just one of the many Canadian artists who have influenced popular music.

audiences. Their concerts, both locally and abroad, consistently draw huge crowds of faithful fans.

One reason for this increased popularity of Canadian artists is because of the federal Canadian content regulations that are followed by radio stations. The CRTC (Canadian Radio-Television and Telecommunications Commission) requires that a minimum of 30 percent of the music played on radio be written or performed by Canadian artists. Much-Music, the nationwide music television station, has also had a positive effect. Canadian performers are showcased through videos, live performances, and interviews.

DANCE

Dance has been a passion of Canadians for many years. Native peoples have used it as a part of their rites for centuries, for the purposes of healing, praying, and celebrating. Today dance has a cross-cultural appeal. Moving to the strains of an Irish jig, a Polish polka, an Italian tarantella, or an Indian Bharata Natyam enables people across the land to express their ethnic heritage.

Ballet has been of special interest in Canada since the 1930s. The country's three top-ranking dance companies are the Royal Winnipeg Ballet, the National Ballet of Canada, and Les Grand Ballets Canadiens. Youngsters attend schools—like Toronto's National Ballet School—from an early age, in hopes of developing their skills and emerging as the next Karen Kain or Veronica Tennant.

Modern dance companies have also come to the fore in recent years. Among the more established are the Paula Ross Company and Anna Wayman Dance Theater of Vancouver, and the Toronto Dance Theater. Peggy Baker, Marie Chouinard, Margie Gillis, Ginette Laurin, and Jean-Pierre Perrault are among the top independent choreographers and dancers of the day.

THE THEATER

Like most of the other arts in Canada, theater did not begin to fully develop until after World War II. While it is true that native peoples have used aspects of ritual drama in religious ceremonies for hundreds of years, more public performances are a relatively recent phenomenon.

The Royal Winnipeg Ballet typically draws large audiences. Ballet is highly respected in Canada, as are other forms of dance.

Prior to 1940, the theater movement was sustained by amateur groups and productions. The Dominion Drama Festival was one of the better known of these. Following the war, thousands of European immigrants poured into Canada, including many skilled in the performing arts. Theater construction increased, and interest began to perk up. Theater in French-speaking Canada developed under the influence of playwright Gratien Gélinas in the 1940s. There were few other stage plays written by Canadians until the next decade.

The movement picked up steam with the establishment of the Stratford Shakespeare Festival in Stratford, Ontario, in 1953. The company—the largest classical theater company in the hemisphere—produces a six-month season of plays. Within a decade, the Shaw Festival was founded, featuring the plays of George Bernard Shaw.

By the 1960s the emphasis had shifted and Canadian plays were beginning to be performed with greater frequency. This was facilitated by the formation of what would later become

The Royal Alexandra Theatre hosts Canadian performances as well as foreign musicals and plays. Interest in the performing arts is on the rise in Canada, resulting in more playwrights and playhouses.

the Playwrights Union of Canada in 1972. Notable playwrights who appeared on the scene included Carol Bolt, Michael Cook, Michel Tremblay, David Fennario, John Murrell, Judith Thompson, Jacques Barbeau, and Guy Sprung.

Since the 1970s interest in the theater has flourished. More and more theaters have emerged, including special-interest ones for children, senior citizens, and feminists. Interest has grown to the point where today, according to recent polls, more Canadians attend performing arts events than sporting events.

MOVIES AND TELEVISION

The Canadian government established the National Film Board in 1939 in an effort to promote films and "to interpret Canada to Canadians and to other countries." It has earned worldwide recognition for its endeavors, having produced more than seventeen thousand films, most of which are documentaries.

To help promote the feature-film industry, the Canadian Film Development Corporation was formed in 1967. This venture has not met with as much success. The film industry in Canada takes a backseat to their U.S. counterparts as far as production is concerned. At present, less than 5 percent of all box-office revenues in Canada are from Canadian films. The Quebec filmmaking industry produced some well-received movies in the 1980s, but lack of funds has prevented more motion pictures from being produced.

"There is no future for an actress in Canada," said Toby Robins in 1968. "The Meccas are elsewhere." For the most part, producers, directors, actors, and actresses who want to make their mark on the big screen have had to do so in the United States. This they have done to no small degree. Louis B. Mayer, Jack Warner, David Cronenberg, and Norman Jewison are Canadians who have achieved success on the production end. Canadians who have realized their dreams in front of the camera include Raymond Burr, John Candy, Jim Carrey, Hume Cronyn, Yvonne DeCarlo, Michael J. Fox, Lorne Greene, Ruby Keeler, Margot Kidder, Kate Nelligan, Leslie Nielsen, Mary Pickford, Walter Pidgeon, Christopher Plummer, Keanu Reeves, William Shatner, Martin Short, and Fay Wray.

Americans might also be surprised to learn that many movies are shot in Canada, such as those in the Superman series. Indeed, Superman, himself, is the creation of Canadian writer Joe Shuster (the *Daily Planet* was modeled after the *Toronto Daily Star*).

Canadian television, like radio, gives "home-grown" performers and writers a boost through the "Canadian content" guidelines of the Canadian Radio-Television and Telecommunications Commission. Sixty percent of all programs must be written or performed by Canadians.

Popular Canadian-born television personalities include Pamela Anderson Lee, Monty Hall, Phil Hartman, Art Linkletter, Rich Little, and Alex Trebek. Lorne Michaels is the brains behind the successful Saturday Night Live program, while Peter Jennings and Morley Safer are television journalists of distinction.

Internationally recognized comedian Jim Carrey hails from Canada. Other Canadian-born funnymen include Leslie Nielsen, Martin Short, and the late John Candy.

SPORTS

Simply put, Canadians are obsessed with hockey. It is the country's favorite spectator sport by far, and one of the most widely played recreational sports. The ultimate dream for most Canadian boys is to someday play at the professional level in America's National Hockey League. Youngsters fantasize about being the next Wayne Gretzky, Gordie Howe, Bobby Orr, Mario Lemieux, or Maurice "The Rocket" Richard. Canada can point with pride to six of the league's franchises—the Montreal Canadians, the Ottawa Senators, the Toronto Maple Leafs, the Calgary Flames, and the Edmonton Oilers. In addition, minor league, college, and high school teams also have their devoted fans who travel from town to town following their favorite team.

Hockey is Canada's most popular sport and continually draws huge crowds of loyal fans. Here, players face off at Calgary's Olympic Saddledome.

The other three major team sports are imports from the United States. Baseball has increased in popularity since the Toronto Blue Jays and Montreal Expos were awarded franchises in the American and National Leagues, respectively. The sport attained its most prominent position when Toronto won the World Series in both 1992 and 1993. In the year prior to Toronto's first championship, pitcher Ferguson Jenkins became the first Canadian elected to the Baseball Hall of Fame.

CIRQUE DU SOLEIL

The École Nationale de Cirque is a special Montreal school for acrobats, trapeze artists, jugglers, actors, and dancers. Students come from all around the world to learn the circus arts and hone their talents. Many dream of qualifying for a position with Montreal's Cirque du Soleil.

The "Circus of the Sun" is like no other circus in the world. The performance is as much a theater production as it is a circus. The all-human cast (there are no animal acts) perform unforgettable acts of skill and daring in a show that is a magical combination of light, music, and sound.

Cirque du Soleil had its beginning in Baie Saint Paul, Quebec, in 1982. A group of young street performers hatched the idea of organizing an entertainers' festival. This soon evolved into the Cirque du Soleil. Cirque's first official show in 1984 coincided with the 450th anniversary of Jacques Cartier's arrival in Canada. From the small town of Gaspé, the troupe went on to perform in cities across the province of Quebec. Greeted with cheers wherever they went, the performers took their acts to the other provinces, then to the United States and, by 1990, to Europe.

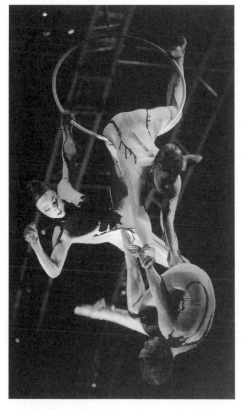

In 1993 Cirque opened its very own theater near the Treasure Island Hotel in Las Vegas. Another permanent show—an aquatic one—is scheduled to open at a new Las Vegas theater in 1998, with other shows to be housed at locations at the Walt Disney World Resort in Orlando, Florida, and in Berlin, Germany, by the year 2000.

Acrobats perform "Aerial Hoops" in the Cirque du Soleil. Many artists aspire to join the Cirque, which has toured Europe and the United States.

Although Canada cannot claim a team in America's National Football League, it does have a professional league of its own. The Canadian Football League consists of teams representing cities all across the country. The championship game to decide the winner of the Grey Cup is a widely covered national event. The most prominent Canadian name in football lore is that of legendary fullback and Rainy River, Ontario, native, Bronko Nagurski.

Interest in basketball is on the climb in Canada, as it is in virtually every country around the globe. The National Basketball Association recently expanded to Canada, awarding franchises to the Toronto Raptors and the Vancouver Huskies. Vancouver natives Bob Houbregs and Pete Newell are both in the Basketball Hall of Fame, as player and college coach, respectively.

Two other sports enjoyed in the Dominion are lacrosse and curling. A version of lacrosse called *baggataway* was played by native peoples prior to the arrival of Europeans in the New World. Comparable to hockey on land, its popularity was such that it was named Canada's official sport upon Confederation in 1867. Curling came over from Scotland and is sometimes referred to as "shuffleboard on ice."

A popular sport in the western reaches of the country is rodeo. The Calgary Stampede, the world's largest rodeo, occupies center stage for ten days each July.

SPORTS HEROES

Calgary was also the site of the 1988 Winter Olympics, while the 1976 Summer games were held in Montreal. Canadian spirits have soared with the triumphs of Olympic medal winners like swimmers Mark Tewksbury and Alex Baumann; skiers Nancy Greene and Kerrin Lee-Gartner; figure skaters Kurt Browning, Barbara Ann Scott, and Elvis Stojko; speed skater Gaétan Boucher; and track star Donovan Bailey. Likewise, the whole country felt the disgrace of Ben Johnson, who lost his gold medal in the 100-meter sprint in the 1988 games after testing positive for illegal drugs.

One special sports hero to Canadians is runner Terry Fox. The young track star was stricken with cancer in the prime of his life and had to have his right leg amputated. Instead of feeling sorry for himself, he set an example for others who have been dealt a

Cancer-stricken runner Terry Fox makes his way across Canada during his "Marathon of Hope." Though he did not finish the journey, his effort was an inspiration to many.

A TIMELY INVENTION

Until just over a hundred years ago, a person traveling across Canada by train had to reset his or her watch to match the local time each time the train made a stop. Twelve o'clock noon was when the sun was directly overhead. When it was noon in Toronto, it was 12:25 in Montreal. Clocks in other towns might say 12:03 or 12:52. In the United States alone, there were a hundred different time zones.

Sandford Fleming, chief engineer of the Canadian Pacific Railway and surveyor of the first rail route across Canada, decided to do something about the situation. His solution was a universal system of time, one that could be used anywhere in the world. He divided a map of the world into twenty-four time zones, each fifteen degrees of longitude wide. Within each zone, the time would be uniform. It would change by one hour when crossing over from one zone to the next.

At first, Fleming's plan was met with resistance. Eventually, however, through his perseverance and persistence, it gained approval at the International Prime Meridian Conference in Washington, D.C. Standard Time went into effect around the world on November 18, 1883.

In addition to developing standardized time zones, Fleming also designed Canada's first postage stamp and promoted the trans-Pacific telegraph cable laid from Vancouver to Australia.

harsh blow in life. He proceeded to attempt a cross-Canada "Marathon of Hope" run to raise money for cancer research. He collapsed before completing the run, however, and less than a year later, on September 1, 1980, he died at the age of twenty-one. An annual Terry Fox Run continues to bring in millions of dollars each year to aid in the fight against this disease.

INVENTIONS AND DISCOVERIES

Canada can lay claim to being the birthplace of a number of innovators whose inventions and discoveries have enriched the world. In the medical field, Dr. Frederick Banting and Charles Best were responsible for the discovery of insulin in 1921. The infant cereal Pablum was developed by Toronto's Hospital for Sick Children around the turn of the century. Another pioneer in the field of science was Belleville-born Herbert Henry Dow, who invented a method for extracting bromine from brine and later established the

Alexander Graham Bell spent part of his life in Nova Scotia. After inventing the telephone, he made the first long-distance phone call on devices hooked up between two Canadian towns.

Dow Chemical Company. Brantford's James Hiller is recognized for designing the first practical electron microscope.

Special mention must also be given to the inventor of the telephone, Alexander Graham Bell. Bell is perhaps the most famous person to have lived in Nova Scotia, having spent many years there after coming over from Scotland at the age of twenty-three. In referring to Canada, he once said, "I have traveled around the globe. I have seen the Canadian and American Rockies, the Andes and the Alps and the Highlands of Scotland; but for simple beauty, Cape Breton outrivals them all." He later moved to the United States but returned to spend many summers doing research in Baddeck. Bell made the first long-distance phone call, from a shoe store in Paris, Ontario, to the town of Brantford, on August 10, 1876.

In a less serious vein, Canadians are also credited with inventing the McIntosh apple (John McIntosh), the banana split (Alfred J. Russell), the chocolate bar (A. D. Ganong), the snowmobile (Joseph-Armand Bombardier), *Canada Dry* ginger ale (John J. McLaughlin), and the paint roller (Norman Breakey). If some of these creations appear trivial, perhaps mention of them can be found in *Trivial Pursuit*, the board game invented by Canadians Chris Haney and Scott Abbott in 1979.

Artistic expression in every field has played an important role in Canada's cultural life. With the support of the government, Canadian originality continues to express itself through the efforts of the men and women who make up the artistic community.

CONTEMPORARY CANADA

5

Canada today faces problems caused by the rapidly changing modern world. No day goes by without word of some new threat to an environment that many people often take for granted. Individual rights are violated, sometimes leading to confrontations that can become violent. The economy fluctuates with conditions often hard to decipher or comprehend. On top of all these, Canada has the ever-present cloud of the separatist movement hanging over its head. "There are two miracles of Canadian history," declared poet F. R. Scott. "The first is the survival of French Canada, and the second is the survival of Canada."

The way these problems are faced will determine the course of the country's future. In order to understand how problems are met and solutions enacted, it is necessary to look at how the government works.

GOVERNMENT

Present-day Canada is composed of ten provinces (Alberta, British Columbia, Manitoba, New Brunswick, Newfoundland, Nova Scotia, Ontario, Prince Edward Island, Quebec, and Saskatchewan) and two territories (Northwest Territories and Yukon Territory). Confederation began with the provisions of the British North America Act in 1867. Complete and total powers to amend the constitution were transferred from the British Parliament to Canada with the passage of the Constitution Act of 1982.

Canada is an independent federal parliamentary state and a self-governing member of the British Commonwealth of Nations. It recognizes Elizabeth II as its sovereign, acting through her appointed governor-general. Both are basically figureheads, however, with the actual power resting with Canada's prime minister.

As a federal state, law-making authority is divided between the central and provincial governments. The central government in the capital city of Ottawa regulates national defense, trade, foreign affairs, immigration, the monetary system, criminal law, and other matters of national import. The provincial and territorial governments take responsibility for concerns that are of greater significance in the daily lives of its citizens, such as education, health, property, civil rights, social security, and the administration of justice.

Ottawa is home to Parliament Hill, which overlooks the Ottawa River. The central government regulates matters of national importance; the territorial governments contend with the daily concerns of the people under their jurisdiction.

The bicameral (two-house) Canadian Parliament consists of a member-appointed Senate patterned after the British House of Lords and a member-elected House of Commons. The 104 members of the Senate, or upper house, are appointed by the governor-general under the recommendation of the prime minister and may serve until age seventy-five. Members are distributed by region of the country rather than by population. The Atlantic Provinces of New Brunswick, Newfoundland, Nova Scotia, and Prince Edward Island are represented by a total of thirty members; Ontario and Quebec, the most heavily populated provinces, have twenty-four each; the western provinces of Alberta, British Columbia, Manitoba, and Saskatchewan have a total of twenty-four; and the Northwest Territories and Yukon Territory have one member each.

THE HOUSE OF COMMONS

In the House of Commons, or lower house, the members are elected to five-year terms by the voters in each constituency (voting district). The number of districts varies with changes in the population. Currently, there are 295 electoral districts. Despite being called the lower house, the House of Commons has far more power than the Senate. Most important bills originate in the lower house, including all those involving taxes and spending money.

The prime minister is the actual head of state in the Canadian government, though the office is not mentioned anywhere in the constitution. Traditionally, the prime minister is the leader of the majority party in the House of Commons. The prime minister holds the position only so long as he or she retains the backing of the majority party.

The prime minister is assisted by a Cabinet, which consists of twenty-five or so members of Parliament whom the

A view inside Parliament's House of Commons. Members of the House of Commons are elected by the people, as opposed to members of the Senate who are appointed by a government official.

Nearly one-quarter of Canada's landscape is covered by forests. Since forestry products help drive the nation's economy, the citizens are very responsive to environmental threats such as acid rain.

prime minister selects from the governing party. These ministers head government departments that manage affairs of agriculture, communications, defense, environment, finance, health and welfare, justice, labor, transportation, and several others.

The provincial and territorial governments are also parliamentary, but with no upper house. In Quebec, the house is known as the National Assembly, while in the other provinces it is called the Legislative Assembly. The actual head of the provincial government is a premier (called the prime minister in Quebec). The two territorial governments have less power than the provincial governments. An elected head official known as the government leader is the top person in the Yukon, while the Northwest Territories is headed by a commissioner appointed by the federal government.

ACID RAIN

The government has to contend with many issues in today's modern, complex world. One of the most pressing is the need to safeguard the environment. People the world over recognize this challenge, and Canadians have taken the matter more seriously than many others.

One of the biggest threats to Canada's ecosystem has been acid deposition, or, as it is better known, acid rain. Acid rain is formed when pollutants are released into the air by the burning of fossil fuels. When these pollutants mix in the atmosphere with nitrogen oxide from automobile emissions, they form secondary pollutants such as nitric acid and sulfuric acid, which are water soluble. The resulting acidic water droplets can be carried great distances by winds and brought back to earth as rain, snow, or fog. This acidic combination can kill both animal and plant life, as well as cause the deterioration of buildings. Since approximately 24 percent of Canadian land is used for forestry and another 7 percent for agriculture, the effects are potentially disastrous. It is estimated that acid rain currently causes $1 billion worth of damage annually in Canada.

Approximately half of the acid rain that falls in Canada is believed to be the end product of combustion originating in industrial plants in the United States. A solution, therefore, requires cooperation between the United States and Canada. Canadian authorities have tightened regulations dealing with emissions, while American authorities have called for more research on the problem. A 1991 accord signed by the two countries committed both to curbing emissions and reducing pollutants. The result has been a drop in acid rain levels since 1995.

U.S.-CANADIAN RELATIONS

The relationship between Canada and the United States remains, as always, a special one. The two countries share the longest undefended border in the world and are close allies as members of the North Atlantic Treaty Organization (NATO). Economically, the United States is the largest investor in Canadian industry and the largest market for Canadian exports.

The degree of closeness between the two nations does lead, however, to occasional problems. One is the perception that the United States tends to exploit its greater power and influence. Canadians are generally considered less assertive and more likely to accept the status quo than their neighbors to the south. As Peter C. Newman notes in his book *Some-*

times a Great Nation: Will Canada Belong to the 21st Century?: "In dramatic contrast to the individualism of the United States, the idea was to be careful, to be plainly dressed, quiet-spoken. . . . You could immediately spot a Canadian at any gathering: he or she was the one who automatically chose the most uncomfortable chair." Indeed, rather than the American goals of "life, liberty and the pursuit of happiness," Canada's first constitution stressed the objectives of "peace, order, and good government."

Traits like compliance and compassion, however, should not be thought of as weaknesses. One of the reasons Canada has been able to survive and prosper as a nation is due to its acceptance and understanding of different cultures.

In the foreword to his book *Canada: A Modern History,* historian J. Bartlet Brebner remarks, "Perhaps the most striking fact about Canada is that it is not part of the United States." Canadians bristle at the implications of such a statement. They do not like being overlooked or taken for granted. When a 1989 Maclean's/Decima poll asked Canadians what they liked least about Americans, the most common response was "superior attitude." Such feelings, however, are probably unavoidable. With the vast majority of its population situated near the U.S. border, most Canadians dress like Americans, speak English, read the same magazines, and watch the same television programs. Americans are not nearly as informed about their neighbors to the north.

Canada and the United States have always been able to settle any disputes between them peacefully. Compromise is a principle well understood by both. Current prime minister Jean Chrétien has demonstrated an ability to disagree with the United States without fear of offending, adding to his popularity and overall acceptance rating among the electorate. As long as common sense and goodwill toward each other continue to be shown, there is every reason to expect the relationship between the countries to remain strong.

THE TREATMENT OF NATIVE PEOPLES AND THE FORMATION OF NUNAVUT

Canada's concern for peace and order extends to its treatment of its first inhabitants. Over the past quarter century, the federal government has encouraged the native peoples of Canada to become absorbed into the society shared by the

CANADIANS IN SPACE

When the United States invited Canada to send an astronaut to fly on one of its space shuttles in 1983, it resulted in the formation of the Canadian Astronaut Program. Out of the four thousand applicants who answered the first call, six were selected—Roberta Bondar, Marc Garneau, Steve MacLean, Ken Money, Bob Thirsk, and Bjarni Tryggvason.

The first Canadian to go up in space was Garneau, who was the payload specialist on Space Shuttle Mission 41-G aboard *Challenger* in October 1984. The job of the payload specialist is to conduct an experiment, or set of experiments, during a mission. The payload is the equipment necessary for the experiments.

The next Canadian to lift off was the country's first woman astronaut, Roberta Bondar. Also a payload specialist, she performed life science and material science experiments in the Spacelab and on the mid-deck aboard *Discovery* in 1992.

Steve MacLean became Canada's third person in space later that same year aboard the space shuttle *Columbia*.

Astronaut Marc Garneau (second row, far right) poses with other members of the 1984 Challenger *crew. Garneau was the first Canadian in space.*

majority of the country's twenty-eight million inhabitants. A large proportion of the half million Indians and Inuit, however, prefer to maintain their cultural and physical isolation from other Canadians. Indian groups have pressed land claims, calling for the return of tribal land taken from them centuries ago. Numerous claims have been settled, while negotiation continues on others.

A move to divide the Northwest Territories was first suggested in the early 1960s. Such division of existing territories was not unheard-of in Canada. The current Northwest Territories was originally part of the larger region known as Rupert's Land when it was purchased from the Hudson's Bay Company in 1869. Manitoba was carved from the region in 1870, the Yukon Territory in 1898, and the provinces of Alberta and Saskatchewan in 1905.

JEAN CHRÉTIEN

The person charged with leading Canada into the future is (Joseph-Jacques) Jean Chrétien. The native of Shawinigan, Quebec, has been one of the country's best-liked politicians for years. Chrétien was the eighteenth of nineteen children born to Wellie Chrétien and Marie Boisvert-Chrétien. He studied law at Laval University and passed the bar in 1958. Five years later he was elected to the House of Commons for the first time. Over the years Chrétien was appointed to nine Cabinet posts. He resigned from the House of Commons and returned to his law practice in 1986. Four years later he was elected as the leader of Canada's Liberal Party. When his party won a majority of seats in the House of Commons in the October 1993 general elections, Chrétien became Canada's twentieth prime minister.

Chrétien has earned a high approval rating for his low-key, down-to-earth style and his reputation for being a man of the people. He has not let his position of power give him an inflated sense of his own importance. "What you see," he has said, "is what you are going to get. . . . The same Chrétien has been running since a few years and I guess there's no discussion about trying to make something different of me."

Chrétien sees Canada's commitment to multiculturalsim as a noble ideal: "Our ability to create unity in diversity is success on which we must continue to build."

A commission appointed by the federal government in the early 1960s decided that division at that time would not be in the best interest of the aboriginal residents of the region. The commission recommended that a system of representative government first be developed in the Northwest Territories. This was done in the late 1960s and 1970s.

In 1976 a proposal that a new territory called Nunavut, to be made from the central and eastern parts of the Northwest Territories, was made by the national Inuit organization called the Inuit Tapirisat of Canada (ITC). That same year, the Déné tribe and the Métis of the western environs proposed a similar division. The new western territory, to be called Denendeh, would guarantee Déné and Métis representation in the Legislative Assembly.

A 1982 vote showed a majority of the electorate in the territories in favor of division. The federal government accepted the idea, subject to certain conditions, such as agreement on boundaries by the parties involved and settlement of Northwest Territories land claims. The Constitutional Alliance was formed in 1982 to negotiate the land claims of the Inuit, Déné, and Métis. It was not until 1990, however, that a

Déné children head home from school. The Déné people of the Northwest Territories are one of the native tribes involved in the partitioning of their province into smaller regions that would ensure their representation in national government.

boundary between the two areas was agreed upon. It was accepted by Inuit voters in a 1992 plebiscite. Government and Inuit representatives signed the final land claim agreement in May 1993.

Nunavut—"Our Land" in the Inuit language of Inuktitut—will officially be taken over by the Inuit government on April 1, 1999. The government will be a public government, representing all residents of Nunavut. The new territory, approximately five times the size of the state of California, will hold the same degree of sovereignty as the other northern territories. Iqaluit has been selected as the territory's capital.

The establishment of Nunavut is important in that it will mark the first time in history that a large area of the northern Canadian lands will be owned by a group of people rather than by the government.

THE SEPARATIST MOVEMENT AND THE CANADIAN IDENTITY

With roots so deeply embedded in the past, it is not likely that Canada will reach a final solution to the issue regarding the rights of the Quebecois. The failures of the Meech Lake

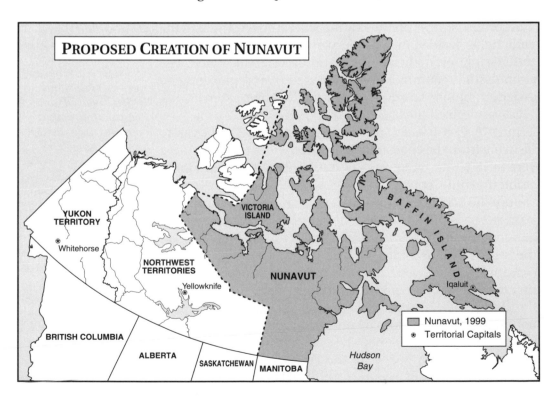

PROPOSED CREATION OF NUNAVUT

and Charlottetown Accords have left both sides with a bitter taste in their mouths. Nearly half the populace in Quebec last voted for independence, so it is naive to think they will be satisfied with maintaining the current state of affairs. On the other hand, many Anglophones outside of Quebec are in effect saying, "Let them go."

This schism remains an obstacle in the pursuit of national unity and, with it, a national identity. Provincial governments are flexing their muscles to a greater degree, and the federal government at times appears at their mercy. The adoption of the Canadian Multiculturalism Act in July 1988 was a step in the right direction. The act asserts that every citizen has an equal chance to participate in every phase of public life, no matter what his or her ethnic background may be. The act gives the government in Ottawa responsibility for promoting multiculturalism throughout all its departments and agencies. In short, it was designed to "encourage and assist the social, cultural, economic and political institutions of Canada to be both respectful and inclusive of Canada's multicultural character." Many provinces have established their own programs and policies to promote multiculturalism as well.

Canada is not a country with a foundation of ethnic conformity like many European and Asian nations. Multiculturalism is a part of the very fabric of Canadian life. The nation's best hope for its future may be its past record of solving its problems with a minimum of radicalism. Despite the obstacles and difficulties that loom on the horizon, Canadians remain proud of their country. More than 90 percent of those interviewed in a 1995 Maclean's-CTV poll stated that "Canada is the best country in the world in which to live." Perhaps this optimism and resolve is the most important attribute of the Canadian identity.

Although some French-Canadians favor separation from anglicized Canada, other citizens of these provinces are trying to work toward unity. Here, two young women participate in an antiseparation rally in Montreal.

FACTS ABOUT CANADA

PROVINCES AND TERRITORIES

Name	Area (sq. mi.)	Population (1993 est.)	Capital
Alberta	255,287	2,662,000	Edmonton
British Columbia	365,948	3,535,000	Victoria
Manitoba	250,947	1,116,000	Winnipeg
New Brunswick	28,355	751,000	Fredericton
Newfoundland	156,649	581,000	Saint John's
Nova Scotia	21,425	923,000	Halifax
Ontario	412,581	10,746,000	Toronto
Prince Edward Island	2,185	132,000	Charlottetown
Quebec	594,860	7,209,000	Quebec City
Saskatchewan	251,866	1,003,000	Regina
Northwest Territories	1,322,910	63,000	Yellowknife
Yukon Territory	186,661	32,000	Whitehorse
TOTAL	3,849,674	28,753,000	

PRIME MINISTERS OF CANADA

Name	Party	Term
Sir John A. Macdonald	Conservative	July 1867–Nov. 1873
Alexander Mackenzie	Liberal	Nov. 1873–Oct. 1878
Sir John A. Macdonald	Conservative	Oct. 1878–June 1891
Sir John J. C. Abbott	Conservative	June 1891–Nov. 1892
Sir John S. D. Thompson	Conservative	Dec. 1892–Dec. 1894
Sir Mackenzie Bowell	Conservative	Dec. 1894–Apr. 1896
Sir Charles Tupper	Conservative	May 1896–July 1896
Sir Wilfrid Laurier	Liberal	July 1896–Oct. 1911
Sir Robert L. Borden	Conservative	Oct. 1911–Oct. 1917
Sir Robert L. Borden	Unionist	Oct. 1917–July 1920
Arthur Meighen	Cons./Unionist	July 1920–Dec. 1921
William Mackenzie King	Liberal	Dec. 1921–June 1926
Arthur Meighen	Conservative	June 1926–Sept. 1926
William Mackenzie King	Liberal	Sept. 1926–Aug. 1930
Richard B. Bennett	Conservative	Aug. 1930–Oct. 1935

Name	Party	Term
William L. Mackenzie King	Liberal	Oct. 1935–Nov. 1948
Louis Stephen St. Laurent	Liberal	Nov. 1948–June 1957
John G. Diefenbaker	Progressive Cons.	June 1957–Apr. 1963
Lester Bowles Pearson	Liberal	Apr. 1963–Apr. 1968
Pierre Elliott Trudeau	Liberal	Apr. 1968–June 1979
Charles Joseph Clark	Progressive Cons.	June 1979–Mar. 1980
Pierre Elliott Trudeau	Liberal	Mar. 1980–June 1984
John Napier Turner	Liberal	June 1984–Sept. 1984
Martin Brian Mulroney	Progressive Cons.	Sept. 1984–June 1993
Kim Campbell	Progressive Cons.	June 1993–Nov. 1993
Jean Chrétien	Liberal	Nov. 1993–

DEMOGRAPHY

Population (1995): 29,463,000; world rank, 32nd

Population density per square mile (1995): 8.3

Urban-rural (1993): urban, 76.7 percent; rural, 23.3 percent

Sex distribution (1993): male, 49.54 percent; female, 50.46 percent

Age breakdown (1993): under 15, 30.7 percent; 15–29, 22.1 percent; 30–44, 25.3 percent; 45–59, 15.9 percent; 60–74, 11.2 percent; 75 and over, 4.8 percent

Population projection: (2000) 31,029,000; (2010) 33,946,000

Ethnic origin (1991): French, 22.8 percent; British, 20.8 percent; German, 3.4 percent; Italian, 2.8 percent; Chinese, 2.2 percent; Amerindian and Inuktitut (Inuit), 1.7 percent; Ukrainian, 1.5 percent; Dutch, 1.3 percent; multiple origin and other, 43.5 percent

Religious affiliation (1991): Roman Catholic, 45.7 percent; Protestant, 36.3 percent; Eastern Orthodox, 1.5 percent; Jewish, 1.2 percent; Muslim, 1.0 percent; Buddhist, 0.7 percent; Hindu, 0.6 percent; nonreligious, 12.4 percent; other, 0.6 percent

Major metropolitan areas (1991): Toronto, 3,893,046; Montreal, 3,127,242; Vancouver, 1,602,502; Ottawa-Hull, 920,857; Edmonton, 839,924; Calgary, 754,033; Winnipeg, 652,354; Quebec, 645,550; Hamilton, 599,760; London, 381,522

Place of birth (1986): 84.2 percent native born; 15.8 percent foreign born—of which United Kingdom, 3.2 percent, other European, 6.6 percent, Asian countries, 3.2 percent, other, 2.8 percent

Birth rate per 1,000 population (1994): 13.1 (world avg. 25.0)

Death rate per 1,000 population (1994): 7.2 (world avg. 9.3)

Natural increase rate per 1,000 population (1994): 5.9 (world avg. 15.7)

Marriage rate per 1,000 population (1992–93): 4.5

Divorce rate per 1,000 population (1992–93): 1.7

Life expectancy at birth (1994): male, 74.7 years; female, 81.7 years

LAND

Land area: 3,849,674 square miles; world rank, 2nd

Land use (1993): forested, 53.6 percent; meadows and pastures, 3.0 percent; agricultural and under permanent cultivation, 4.9 percent; built on, wasteland, and other, 38.5 percent

Highest point: Mount Logan, 19,850 feet

Largest island: Baffin, 195,928 square miles

Largest lake: Great Bear, 12,096 square miles

NATIONAL ECONOMY

Gross national product (1993): US $574,936,000,000

Budget (1992–93): Revenue: CAN $140,981,000,000 (income taxes, 54.3 percent; sales tax, 21.0 percent; import duties, 2.6 percent). Expenditures: CAN $170,019,000,000 (public debt interest, 23.3 percent; defense, 7.0 percent; health, 4.5 percent; education, 2.6 percent; foreign assistance, 2.2 percent)

National debt (1990–91): CAN $443,278,000,000

Household income and expenditures (1991): Average household size, 2.8; average annual income per family, US $45,261

Imports (1993): CAN $169,316,000,000 (machinery and transport equipment, 54.9 percent—of which motor vehicles, 23.5 percent; food, feed, beverages, and tobacco, 6.5 percent; petroleum and energy products, 4.1 percent; forestry products, 0.9 percent). Major import sources: United States, 65.0 percent; Japan, 6.1 percent; United Kingdom, 2.6 percent; Mexico, 2.2 percent; Germany, 2.0 percent; China, 1.8 percent; France, 1.3 percent; Italy, 1.1 percent; South Korea, 0.9 percent; Norway, 0.6 percent

Exports (1993): CAN $181,026,000,000 (machinery and transport equipment, 39.4 percent—of which motor vehicles, 26.2 percent; mineral fuels, 10.5 percent—of which crude petroleum, 3.7 percent; food, 6.4 percent—of which wheat, 1.5 percent; lumber, 5.0 percent; newsprint, 3.2 percent; wood pulp, 2.5 percent; office equipment, 2.5 percent; aluminum, 2.0 percent; refined petroleum products, 1.4 percent). Major export destinations: United States, 81.3 percent; Japan, 4.6 percent; United Kingdom, 1.5 percent; Germany, 1.3 percent; China, 0.9 percent; South Korea, 0.9 percent; Netherlands, 0.7 percent; Italy, 0.7 percent; France, 0.6 percent; Mexico, 0.4 percent

CHRONOLOGY

B.C.

ca. 1300
First Asians cross into North America

A.D.

ca. 1000
Vikings arrive in Newfoundland and establish settlement at L'Anse-aux-Meadows

1497
John Cabot lands on east coast of Canada

1534
Jacques Cartier discovers the Gulf of Saint Lawrence

1576
Martin Frobisher searches for the Northwest Passage

1603
Samuel de Champlain makes first voyage to Canada

1605
French settlers establish Port Royal in what is now Nova Scotia

1608
Champlain establishes Quebec City at Indian site on Saint Lawrence River

1610
Henry Hudson discovers Hudson Bay

1627
Company of New France established

1632
Champlain appointed first governor of Canada

1642
French settlers found Montreal

1670
Hudson's Bay Company chartered

1689–1763
British capture Quebec and defeat New France

1755
Expulsion of Acadians from Nova Scotia

1758
Louisbourg falls to British

1759
British defeat French at Quebec on Plains of Abraham

1760–1777
Eight thousand pro-Loyalist New England planters arrive in Canada

1763
Treaty of Paris formally cedes Canada to Great Britain

1769
Colony of Saint John's Island (renamed Prince Edward Island in 1799) established

1774
Quebec Act grants political and religious rights to French Canadians

1783
North West Company of fur traders established

1784
Colony of New Brunswick established

1791
Province of Quebec divided into Upper Canada and Lower Canada by Constitutional Act (Canada Act)

1793
Alexander Mackenzie reaches Pacific Ocean

1812

Lord Selkirk establishes settlement at Red River in Manitoba

1818

Forty-ninth parallel accepted as boundary between the United States and Canada for area between Lake of the Woods and Rocky Mountains

1821

Hudson's Bay Company and North West Company amalgamated

1836

First railway line joins Laprairie and Saint-Jean-sur-Richelieu

1837–1838

Rebellions against government break out in Upper and Lower Canada

1839

Lord Durham urges self-government for Canada in report to Queen Victoria

1840

Act of Union unites Upper and Lower Canada under one governor and legislature

1846

Western boundary between United States and Canada extended from Rockies to Pacific coast by Oregon Treaty

1858

Fraser River gold rush begins

1866

United Colony of British Columbia created

1867

British North America Act creates Dominion of Canada with four provinces—Ontario, Quebec, Nova Scotia, and New Brunswick

1867–1873
Conservatives form first federal government under John A. Macdonald

1869
Dominion of Canada purchases western lands from Hudson's Bay Company

1869–1870
Louis Riel leads Métis rebellion on Canadian prairies

1870
Manitoba becomes province

1871
British Columbia becomes province

1873
Conservatives resign following Pacific Scandal involving railway kickbacks

1873–1878
Liberals come to power under Alexander Mackenzie

1873
Prince Edward Island becomes province

1873
North-West Mounted Police established

1878–1896
Conservatives reelected under John A. Macdonald

1885
North West Rebellion on prairies; Louis Riel executed; transcontinental railroad (Canadian Pacific) is completed

1896
Discovery of gold in Klondike spurs Yukon gold rush

1896–1911
Liberal Party elected under Wilfrid Laurier

1905
Alberta and Saskatchewan become provinces

1911–1917
Conservatives elected under Robert Borden

1914–1918
More than 600,000 Canadians serve in Allied forces in
World War I; more than 60,000 die

1917
Military Service Act becomes law, introducing conscrip-
tion; women given the right to vote; establishment of
Canadian National Railway

1917–1921
Election of Unionist government under Robert Borden

1919
Winnipeg General Strike

1921
Liberals elected under William Lyon Mackenzie King

1926
In Britain, Balfour Report recognizes dominions, including
Canada, as autonomous nations

1930–1935
Conservatives under R. B. Bennett are elected

1931
Statute of Westminster gives Canada complete independence from Great Britain

1935–1957
Liberals elected under William Lyon Mackenzie King

1939–1945
More than 1,000,000 Canadians serve in World War II; almost 100,000 die

1945
Canada becomes founding member of United Nations

1948
Louis St. Laurent succeeds William Lyon Mackenzie King as
prime minister

1949
Newfoundland becomes tenth province; Canada, United States, and ten Western European nations form North American Treaty Organization (NATO)

1954–1959
Canada and United States build Saint Lawrence Seaway, making Great Lakes accessible to seagoing vessels

1957–1963
Progressive Conservatives elected under John G. Diefenbaker

1957
Lester Pearson wins Nobel Peace Prize; United States and Canada sign North American Air Defense Command (NORAD) agreement

1960
Quebec's new Liberal government undertakes measures marking beginning of the Quiet Revolution

1963–1968
Liberals elected under Lester Pearson

1965
Canada's maple leaf flag replaces Red Ensign

1967
Canada celebrates its centennial (one hundred years since Confederation); Expo 67 held in Montreal

1968–1979
Liberals elected under Pierre Elliott Trudeau

1969
Canada's Parliament passes Official Languages Act, making country officially bilingual

1970
October Crisis in Quebec; War Measures Act is invoked

1974
Quebec's National Assembly adopts Bill 22, making French the province's official language

1976

Parti Québecois, led by René Lévesque, wins election to run provincial government in Quebec on platform promising to seek separation from Canada; Olympic Games held in Montreal

1979–1980

Progressive Conservatives elected under Joe Clark

1980

Quebec referendum on "sovereignty-association" is defeated

1981

Federal government and all provinces except Quebec reach agreement on bringing Canada's Constitution home from British Parliament

1982

Patriation officially occurs on April 17 in Ottawa as Queen Elizabeth II officially proclaims Canada's own constitution (Constitution Act)

1984–1993

Progressive Conservatives elected under Brian Mulroney

1986

Expo 86 held in Vancouver

1987

Prime Minister Brian Mulroney and ten provincial premiers agree on major amendments to constitution in Meech Lake Accord

1988

1988 Winter Olympics held in Calgary, Alberta; Free Trade Agreement signed between Canada and United States

1990

Meech Lake Accord dies two provinces short of unanimous ratification

1992

Charlottetown Accord rejected by six of ten provinces

1993

Brian Mulroney resigns as prime minister; Kim Campbell sworn in as Canada's first woman prime minister; Canada approves North American Free Trade Agreement (NAFTA)

1993-1997

Liberals elected under Jean Chrétien

1995

Quebec rejects referendum on sovereignty

SUGGESTIONS FOR FURTHER READING

Adam Bryant, *Canada: Good Neighbor to the World.* Minneapolis, MN: Dillon Press, 1987. This book in the Discovering Our Heritage series is a general overview of Canadian life aimed at young readers. A chapter on living and eating in Canada features several recipes for local foods.

Canada in Pictures. Minneapolis, MN: Lerner, 1989. Dozens of color and black-and-white photos will make this addition to the Visual Geography series visually appealing to young readers.

Robert Carse, *The High Country.* New York: W. W. Norton, 1966. An interesting book describing the early explorations of Canada. The adventures and hardships faced by Pierre Radisson, Robert Rogers, James Cook, Alexander Mackenzie, and others are recounted in detail.

Michael Cooper, *Klondike Fever.* New York: Clarion Books, 1989. The hopes and dreams of those who came to the Klondike in hopes of finding gold are described in this nicely illustrated volume for youngsters.

Bobbie Kalman, *Canada the Land; Canada the People;* and *Canada the Culture.* New York: Crabtree, 1993. Numerous color photographs enhance these three volumes in the Lands, Peoples, and Cultures series. These very attractive books focus on life in modern-day Canada.

Kevin Law, *Places and Peoples of the World: Canada.* New York: Chelsea House, 1990. This volume in the Places and Peoples of the World series is an easy-to-read history of Canada. Basic information on Canadian government, economy, and culture is also provided.

Andrew H. Malcolm, *The Canadians.* New York: Times Books, 1985. Malcolm's look at Canada focuses on the land and its inhabitants. In observing Canadians at home, at work, and at play, the author helps us better understand the people, their minds, and their land.

————, *The Land and People of Canada*. New York: Harper-Collins, 1991. This volume in the Portraits of the Nations series attempts to answer the question "Who are the Canadians?" by looking at the diverse lifestyles and histories of the people that comprise this vast nation.

Benton and Louise Minks, *The French and Indian War*. San Diego: Lucent Books, 1995. Part of the World History series, this book presents a comprehensive overview of the conflicts between the French and English in North America. Numerous quotes from primary sources bring the period to life in an interesting way.

Richard Morenus, *The Hudson's Bay Company*. New York: Random House, 1956. This book for young people presents an interesting overview of the lives of fur trappers in the Hudson Bay region.

Delia Ray, *Gold! The Klondike Adventure*. New York: E. P. Dutton, 1989. Numerous rare photographs enhance this enjoyable volume on the Klondike gold rush. The book is sure to hold the interest of young readers looking for an account of the last great adventure in North American history.

Works Consulted

Robert Bothwell, Ian Drummond, and John English, *Canada 1900–1945*. Toronto: University of Toronto Press, 1987. A detailed record of the events affecting Canadian life in the first half of the twentieth century. The political and economic forces that shaped the period are analyzed.

———, *Canada Since 1945*. Toronto: University of Toronto Press, 1989. This work highlights the changes undergone by Canada in the period following World War II. The governments of St. Laurent, Diefenbaker, Pearson, and Trudeau are focused upon.

J. Bartlet Brebner, *Canada: A Modern History.* Ann Arbor: University of Michigan Press, 1960. A thorough documentation of Canadian history is given in this volume from the University of Michigan History of the Modern World series.

Olive Patricia Dickason, *Canada's First Nations*. Norman: University of Oklahoma Press, 1992. An excellent history of the native peoples of Canada. The Amerindian and Inuit struggle to preserve their culture in the modern world is well chronicled.

Peter C. Newman, *Sometimes a Great Nation: Will Canada Belong to the 21st Century?* Toronto: McClelland and Stewart, 1988. As the title suggests, this book discusses the uncertain future of Canada.

Wayne C. Thompson, *Canada 1994*. Harpers Ferry, WV: Stryker-Post, 1995. This volume in the World Today series gives a very good overview of Canadian history up to the present day. The Canadian political system is also examined in great detail.

William Toye, *The St. Lawrence*. New York: Henry Z. Walck, 1959. Photographs and illustrations enhance this account of the history of the world's greatest inland waterway.

INDEX

Abbott, Scott, 80
Acadia, 19, 20
acid rain, 85
African Canadians, 48
agriculture, 31, 36, 49, 61
Alberta, 11, 81, 83, 93
  attractions in, 61, 69
  ethnic groups in, 44, 47
  history of, 27, 88
  natural resources in, 36
  see also Calgary; Edmonton
Algonquian Indians, 10, 14, 44
Anglophones, 42, 91
Anne of Green Gables (Montgomery), 70
architecture, 68–69
art, 66–68
Asian Canadians, 47–48, 52, 53
Assiniboin Indians, 30, 44
Astronaut Program, Canadian, 87
Atwood, Margaret, 70

baggataway (lacrosse), 78
Banting, Frederick, 79
baseball, 76
basketball, 78
Bell, Alexander Graham, 80
Bella Coola Indians, 11, 44
Bellow, Saul, 70
Bennett, Richard, 35
Beothuk Indians, 10
Berton, Pierre, 70
Best, Charles, 79
Bickert, Ed, 71
Blackfoot Indians, 11, 44
Blais, Marie Claire, 70
Blood Indians, 11
Bluenose (schooner), 62
Bombardier, Joseph-Armand, 80
Borden, Robert, 32
Borduas, Paul-Émile, 67
British Canadians. *See* English Canadians
British Columbia, 11, 81, 83, 93
  attractions in, 61
  ethnic groups in, 47
  history of, 29–31
British Commonwealth of Nations, 34, 81
British Crown. *See* England

British North American Act, 26, 27, 56, 81
Brooke, Francis, 70
Brown, George, 25–26
Buade, Louis de, Comte de Frontenac, 19

Cabot, John (Giovanni Caboto), 12
Calgary, Alberta, 54, 76, 78
Campbell, Kim, 42
Canada, 93-95
  American Civil War and, 25
  British Emancipation Act and, 48
  Confederation of, 25–30, 46, 65, 81
  Dominion of, 26–28, 31
  economy of, 34–39, 41, 60–61, 95
  European explorers in, 11–13, 14–15, 17–18
  flags of, 38, 39
  multiculturalism in, 47–48, 88, 91
  naming of, 13
  prehistoric settlers in, 9
  Upper/Lower divisions of, 23, 24–25, 27
  urbanization of, 48–51
  see also Canadian government; United States
Canada East/West, 27
Canadian Film Development Corporation, 74
Canadian Football League, 77
Canadian government, 81–84
  British Commonwealth of Nations and, 34, 81
  British North American Act and, 26, 27, 56, 81
  Canada Council of, 64
  Charlottetown Accord of, 42, 90–91
  Conservative Party of, 25–27, 31–32, 35, 42
  Constitution Act of, 41, 81
  Constitutional Alliance of, 89–90
  Constitution and Charter of Rights and Freedoms of, 41
  Family Allowances Act of, 59–60
  Free Trade Agreement (FTA) and, 41
  House of Commons, 27, 83, 88
  Human Rights Act of, 48
  Indian Act of, 43
  League of Nations and, 32

Legislative Assembly of, 84, 89
Liberal Party of, 25–26, 34–35,
    37–38, 42, 88
Meech Lake Accord of, 41–42, 90–91
native peoples and, 86, 88–90
North Atlantic Treaty Organization
    and, 36–37, 85
Official Languages Act of, 40
Parliament of, 27, 41–42, 45, 83–84
Pension Plan of, 38
Progressive Conservatives of,
    37–38, 41
Reformer Party of, 25–26
Senate, 27, 83
Student Loan Program of, 56
Treaty of Versailles and, 32
War Measures Act of, 40
Canadian Opera Company, 71
Canadian Radio-Television and
    Telecommunications Commission,
    72, 75
Cape Breton Island, 19–21
Carmack, George Washington, 33
Carmichael, Franklin, 66
Carr, Emily, 67
Cartier, George Étienne, 24–25
Cartier, Jacques, 12–13, 77
Catholics (French), 23, 46, 55, 58
Cavelier, Robert, Sieur de La Salle,
    17–18
Cayuga Indians, 10
Champlain, Samuel de, 14, 16
Charles II (king of England), 17
Charlottetown Accord (1992), 42,
    90–91
Chinese Canadians, 47, 52, 53, 66
Chouinard, Marie, 72
Chrétien, Jean, 42, 86, 88
Christianity, 58, 59, 64–65
    missionaries of, 14, 17–18, 51
Cirque du Soleil, 77
Colebourn, Harry, 35
Columbus, Christopher, 12–13
Colville, Alexander, 68
Company of the Hundred Associates,
    15–16
Cook, Michael, 74
coureurs de bois (fur traders), 16
Cree Indians, 10, 11, 44
curling, 78

dance, 72
Davidson, Robert, 68
Davies, Robertson, 70
Davies, Thomas, 66
Déné Indians, 44, 89
Denendeh, 89
Desmarais, Lorraine, 71
Diefenbaker, John, 38
Donato, Michel, 71

Dow, Herbert Henry, 79–80

Edmonton, Alberta, 53–54, 66, 69, 76
education, 56–58
England, 15, 16
    Act of Union and, 25
    control of Canada and, 24–25, 27,
        32, 34
    explorers of, 12, 14–15
    Loyalists of, 23, 46
    Quebec Act of 1774 and, 22–23
    Statute of Westminster and, 34
    wars of, 16, 18–22
English Canadians, 6, 39, 46
    as Anglophones, 42, 91
    World War I and, 32
    World War II and, 36
Erickson, Arthur, 68, 69
Ericson, Leif, 11
Eskimos. See Inuit people
European explorers, 11–13, 14–15,
    17–18

farming. See agriculture
Film Board, National, 74
Film Development Corporation,
    Canadian, 74
filmmaking industry, 74–75
First Nations, 43–44, 86, 88
fishing industry, 12, 13, 15, 61
flags, 38, 39
football, 77–78
forestry, 61, 85
forts, 28, 30
Fox, Terry, 78–79
France, 15–16, 18
    explorers from, 12–13, 17–18
    fur trade of, 13–14, 16
    seigneurial system of, 16
    wars of, 16, 18–22
Francis I (king of France), 12
francophones, 71–72
Fraser, Simon, 24
Fréchette, Louis Honoré, 70
Free Trade Agreement (FTA), 41
French and Indian War, 21
French Canadians, 6, 22, 39, 46, 55
    culture of, 51–52, 54–55
    La Conquête and, 21
    separatist movement of, 40–42, 46,
        55, 81, 90–91
    as slave owners, 48
    World War I and, 32
    World War II and, 36
Front de Libération du Québec
    (FLQ), 40
fur trading, 13–14, 16–17, 23–24
    centers for, 51, 55

Garneau, Marc, 87

Gaucher, Yves, 68
Gélinas, Gratien, 73
German Canadians, 47
glaciers, 9, 10–11
gold mining, 29, 33, 47
Great Britain. *See* England
Gretzky, Wayne, 76
Groseilliers, Médard Chouart des, 16–17
Group of Seven, 66–67

Haida Indians, 11, 44
Haliburton, T. C., 70
Halifax, Nova Scotia, 55–56
Haney, Chris, 80
Harris, Lawren, 66
health care, 59
Hébert, Anne, 70
Henderson, Robert, 33
Henry IV (king of France), 14
Henry VII (king of England), 12
Hiller, James, 80
Histoire de la Nouvelle France (Lescarbot), 69–70
hockey, 75–76
holidays, 64–66
Houbregs, Bob, 78
Hudson, Henry, 14–15
Hudson Bay, 15, 18, 19
Hudson's Bay Company, 17, 23–24, 27, 88
Huron Indians, 14, 16, 44

immigration, 24, 31, 36, 46–50, 55, 73
Indian people, 43–44, 50, 88
    carvings of, 68
    children of, 56
Innu people, 50
Inuit Circumpolar Conference, 45
Inuit people, 13, 44–45, 51, 88–90
    assimilation of, 6, 50, 88
    carvings of, 68
    children of, 56, 65
    history of, 9
Inuit Tapirisat of Canada (ITC), 89
Inuktitut, 90
inventions, 79–80
Iqaluit, 90
Iroquois Indians, 10, 44
    Canadian history and, 13, 14, 16, 21, 65
Isle Royale, 19
Italian Canadians, 47

Jackson, Alexander Young, 66
Jenkins, Ferguson, 76
Johnson, Ben, 78
Johnston, Franz, 66

Kane, Paul, 66

Kerouac, Jack, 70
King, William Lyon Mackenzie, 34–36
King George's War, 20
Kirby, William, 70
Kootenay Indians, 11
Krieghoff, Cornelius, 66
Kwakiutl Indians, 44

labor history, 32–33
La Conquête, 21
lacrosse, 78
Lambton, John, Earl of Durham, 25
Laporte, Pierre, 40
La Salle, Sieur. *See* Cavelier, Robert
Laurier, Wilfred, 31–32
Lavoie, Daniel, 71–72
Lawrence, Charles, 20
League of Canadian Poets, 70
Légaré, Joseph, 66
Lemieux, Jean-Paul, 67
Lesage, Jean, 39
Lescarbot, Marc, 69–70
Lévesque, René, 40
Lillooet Indians, 11
Lismer, Arthur, 66
literature, 69–70
Livesay, Dorothy, 70
Longfellow, Henry Wadsworth, 20
Louis XIV (king of France), 16
Lower/Upper Canada, 23, 24–25, 27
Luc, Frère, 66

MacDonald, James Edward Hervey, 66
Macdonald, John A., 25–31
Mackenzie, Alexander, 24, 30
Mackenzie, William Lyon, 24–25
MacLennan, Hugh, 46, 70
Maillet, Antonine, 70
Maliseet Indians, 44
Manitoba, 11, 42, 81, 83, 93
    attractions of, 62
    ethnic groups of, 44, 47
    history of, 27–29, 88
    see also Winnipeg
Maritime Provinces, 9–10, 26
Marquette, Jacques, 17–18
Massey, Geoffrey, 69
Mayer, Louis B., 75
McIntosh, John, 80
McLaughlin, John J., 80
Meech Lake Accord, 41–42, 90–91
Métis, 27–29, 43, 44, 89
Micmac Indians, 10, 44
Milne, A. A., 35
Milne, David, 67
mining industry, 31
Miquelon Island, 22
missionaries, 14, 17–18, 51
Mohawk Indians, 10, 14

Molinari, Guido, 68
Montcalm, Louis Joseph de, 21
Montgomery, Lucy Maud, 70
Montreal, 21, 25, 51–52
    attractions in, 51, 58, 71, 76, 77
    automatiste movement in, 67
    ethnic groups in, 47
    Expo 67 in, 52, 69
Morissette, Alanis, 71
Moriyama, Raymond, 69
movies, 74–75
Mulroney, Brian, 41–42
multiculturalism, 47–48, 88, 91
Munro, Alice, 70
Murray, Robert, 68
Murrell, John, 74
music, 70–72

National Basketball Association, 78
National Film Board, 74
Nelligan, Émile, 70

New Brunswick, 9–10, 81, 83, 93
    attractions in, 62
    early history of, 12–13, 23, 26, 27
Newell, Pete, 78
Newfoundland, 9–10, 42, 61, 81, 83,
    93
    history of, 11–12, 19, 26, 36
    holidays in, 66
New France, 14, 15–17, 19–20, 22, 48
Newman, Peter C., 85–86
Nootka Indians, 11
North Atlantic Treaty Organization
    (NATO), 36–37, 85
North West Company, 23–24
North-West Mounted Police, 30, 54
Northwest Territories, 56, 81, 83, 84,
    93
    attractions in, 62
    division of, 88–89
    history of, 27, 31
    see also Inuit people
Nova Scotia, 9–10, 81, 83, 93
    attractions in, 62
    Bluenose and, 62
    ethnic groups in, 47
    history of, 12, 19, 20, 23, 26, 27
    see also Halifax
Nunavut, 89–90

Ojibwa Indians, 10, 44
Olympic competitions, 52, 54, 62, 78
Oneida Indians, 10
Ontario, 30, 37, 60, 81, 83, 93
    attractions in, 62, 67, 69, 73
    ethnic groups in, 24, 47
    history of, 23, 26, 27, 31
    see also Toronto
Opera Company, Canadian, 71

Ormeaux, Dollard des, 65
Ottawa, Ontario, 52, 82
    attractions of, 53, 54, 66, 69, 76

Papineau, Louis Joseph, 24
Parizeau, Jacques, 42
Parkin, John C., 69
parks, 61–62
Pearson, Lester Bowles, 38, 40
Pei, I. M., 69
Perrault, Jean-Pierre, 72
Peterson, Oscar, 71
Piergan Indians, 11
Plains Indians, 11, 30
Playwrights Union of Canada, 73–74
Poets, League of Canadian, 70
polls, 86, 91
Pontiac Indians, 18
prime ministers, 81, 83–84, 93–94
    Bennett, 35
    Borden, 32
    Cabinet members and, 83–84
    Campbell, 42
    Chrétien, 42, 86, 88
    Diefenbaker, 38
    King, 34–35
    Laurier, 31–32
    Macdonald, 27–31
    Mackenzie, 30
    Mulroney, 41–42
    Pearson, 38, 40
    St. Laurent, 36–37
    Trudeau, 40–41
Prince Edward Island, 9–10, 81, 83, 93
    history of, 26, 30
Protestants (British), 23, 46

Quebec, 9–10, 30, 37, 60, 81, 83, 93
    education in, 57
    government of, 39–42, 84
    history of, 14, 19, 21–23, 26, 27
    holidays in, 66
    Parti Québecois (PQ) in, 40, 42, 46
    riots in, 36
    see also French Canadians; Mon-
    treal; Quebec City; Quebecers/Que-
    becois
Quebec Act of 1874, 22–23
Quebec City, 13, 16, 54–55
    attractions in, 7, 66
Quebecers/Quebecois, 39–40, 55,
    90–91
    Quiet Revolution of, 46, 51–52
Queen Anne's War, 19

Rabinovitch, David, 68
Radio-Television and Telecommuni-
    cations Commission, Canadian
    (CRTC), 72, 75
Radisson, Pierre Esprit, 16–17

railroads, 25, 29–31, 47, 52, 55
Reagan, Ronald, 8
Reaney, James, 71
religion, 58, 59, 64–65
révolution tranquille (Quiet Revolution), 46
Richard, Maurice, 76
Richardson, John, 70
Riel, Louis, 28–29
ringette (sport), 62
Roberts, Charles G. D., 70
rodeos, 78
Roy, Gabrielle, 70
Royal Canadian Mounted Police (RCMP), 30, 33
Rupert (prince of England), 17
Rupert's Land, 17, 27, 88
Russell, Alfred J., 80

Saint Lawrence River, 20, 51
   European explorers on, 12–13, 14, 21
Saint Lawrence Seaway, 37, 38
Saint Pierre Island, 22
Salish Indians, 11
Saskatchewan, 11, 81, 83, 93
   attractions in, 62
   ethnic groups in, 47
   history of, 27, 88
schools, 56–58, 68
   French-immersion, 57
Scott, Thomas, 26–27
Secord, Laura Ingersoll, 26
Seneca Indians, 10
separatist movement, 40–42, 46, 55, 81, 90–91
Shadbolt, Jack, 68
Shushwap Indians, 11
Shuster, Joe, 75
Sioux Indians, 11
Slavey Indians, 44
Smith, Gordon, 68
Smith, William B., 62
social service programs, 36, 38, 59–60
   for native peoples, 44, 45
Spain, 19, 22
sports, 62–63, 75–78
   heroes, 78–79
St. Laurent, Louis, 36–37
Stadaconda, 13
steel industry, 32
stock market, 1929 crash, 34–35

Talon, Jean, 16
television, 75
Tennant, Veronica, 72
theater, 72–74, 77
Thompson, David, 24
Thomson, Tom, 66
Thorvaldson, Eric the Red, 11

Toronto, Ontario, 25, 47, 49, 51
   attractions in, 51, 52, 66, 69, 71, 72, 76, 78
Toronto Daily Star, 75
treaties
   of Aix-la-Chapelle, 20
   of Paris, 22
   of Ryswick, 18
   of Saint-Germain-en-Laye, 16
   of Utrecht, 19, 20
   of Versailles, 32
Tremblay, Michel, 74
Trudeau, Pierre Elliott, 6–7, 40–41
Truman, Harry, 37
Tsimshian Indians, 44
Twain, Shania, 71

Ukrainian Canadians, 47, 55
Underground Railroad, 48
United Nations, 36
   Human Development Index, 8
United States, 24, 43, 85–86
   as ally, 36–37
   as colonies, 15, 17–18, 22–23
   emigrants from, 36–37, 54
   influence of, 6–7, 34–35, 64
   sports in, 76–77
   trade with Canada, 31, 41, 85
universities, 58, 68, 69
Upper/Lower Canada, 23, 24–25, 27

Vancouver, British Columbia, 52, 71, 72, 78
Vancouver Island, 29
Vickers, Jon, 71
Victoria (queen of England), 25, 52, 65
Viking explorers, 11
Voisine, Roch, 71–72

War of 1812, 24, 26
War of the Austrian Succession, 20
War of the Grand Alliance, 18, 19
War of the Spanish Succession, 19, 20
Western Cordillera, 11
William III (king of England), 18
Winnie-the-Pooh (Milne), 35
Winnipeg, Manitoba, 28, 35, 55
   attractions in, 72, 73
   general strike in, 33
Winslow, John, 20
Wolfe, James, 21
World War I, 32, 35
World War II, 35–36
Writers' Union of Canada, 70

Young, Karen, 71
Yukon Territory, 31, 56, 81, 83, 84, 93
   attractions in, 62
   history of, 9, 88
   holidays in, 66

PICTURE CREDITS

ABOUT THE AUTHOR

John F. Grabowski is a native of Brooklyn, New York. He holds a bachelor's degree in psychology from City College of New York and a master's degree in educational psychology from Teacher's College, Columbia University. He has been a teacher for twenty-nine years, as well as a freelance writer, specializing in the fields of sports, education, and comedy. His body of published work includes sixteen books; a nationally syndicated sports column; consultation on several math textbooks; articles for newspapers, magazines, and the programs of professional sports teams; and comedy material sold to Jay Leno, Joan Rivers, and numerous other comics. He and his wife, Patricia, live in Staten Island with their daughter, Elizabeth.